True Ghost Stories

Cheiro

FREEWAY PRESS

Kessinger Publishing's Rare Reprints
Thousands of Scarce and Hard-to-Find Books!

- · · ·
- · · ·
- · · ·
- · · ·
- · · ·
- · · ·
- · · ·
- · · ·
- · · ·
- · · ·
- · · ·
- · · ·
- · · ·
- · · ·
- · · ·
- · · ·
- · · ·
- · · ·
- · · ·
- · · ·

We kindly invite you to view our extensive catalog list at:
http://www.kessinger.net

INTRODUCTION

IS there anyone in this wide world who does not believe in ghosts ? Is there any person who has not had at some period of his or her existence, at least one or more mysterious experience that cannot be explained by the ordinary rules governing life ?

I believe the only honest answer to these questions is an emphatic—No.

Among the many thousands of people I have come into close contact with, I have yet to meet the individual who can truthfully say that he or she has never had an experience that does not point to some mysterious influence from " behind the veil " that has come into their life at one time or another.

There are a few persons no doubt who are loth to confess even to their most intimate friends that they believe in such things as ghosts or spirits. They are afraid to be considered " weak-minded " or credulous. They think it sounds brave to say that "such things have never come to them." In their pretence of being strong-minded they lose sight of the fact that from the earliest dawn of history down to the present day, every page contains

7

records that the greatest leaders of mankind in all walks of life have acknowledged that at some time or another they have received warnings, messages or guidance from what is called " the other world " that are beyond all explanation that the practical mind can offer.

To some, these experiences may be of rare occurrence. To others, they come at varying intervals, while again to others they are almost commonplace in the frequency of their manifestations.

Why this should be so is one of the mysteries of life. It may be explained by the varying magnetism or electric forces radiating from each individual. It may be due to a thousand and one causes, but the fact remains that all human beings at some time or another have occult experiences while treading Life's pathway from the Cradle to the Grave.

It would be outside my province in a book of this kind to enter into various arguments that could be brought forward to support the theory that life, as we know it, is but the forepart of that greater life that only opens for us as the Gates of Death are closing on the world we leave behind.

If I did enter into such arguments, I might be in danger of perhaps hurting the religious sentiments of some, or antagonising others, by the views I might be forced to express.

Such is not the object of this book—it is not written in any contentious spirit. It is not written for any special class of thinker, but simply for the general public—a plain unvarnished account of my own experiences in connection with such matters and nothing more.

The only merit of the following pages are that they contain—*True Ghost Stories*—either from my own personal experience or related to me by those whom I have every reason to believe were telling me the truth.

I have given to them the simple title of Ghost Stories, because the word " Ghost " has been in common use for centuries. In many cases the title " Spirit " might have been more appropriate, but had I used this word, I would have probably been classed as one of the many writers who are avowed Spiritualists, and prejudice might prevent this book from reaching the general public for which it is intended.

It is only fair to my readers to state clearly and emphatically that I do not belong to any Psychological Society or organisation whatsoever. I am, rightly or wrongly, not a Member of any Church, nor do I belong to any religious body, or congregation of any sort of conventional religion.

While not acknowledging any form of worship " as the only true one," I respect *the underlying purpose of all.* At the same time, and with just as much earnestness as any religious devotee, I hold to my independence of thought as the most suitable for my individual needs. As a believer in the Creator of all things, I bow before the Infinite Wisdom that permits the growth of various creeds to suit the varying types of humanity that have been called into existence.

If some of these require for their faith altars of gold, carved cathedrals, pomp of priests, or the whitewashed walls of Puritans, I humbly recognise in all the plan of Divine Design that has created all, and ask only for myself, that I be allowed the same liberty to worship my God in my own way under the stars of Night or the Mid-day Sun, or find His words in flowers and trees and stones, and in everyday acts of self-denial that like a thread of gold run through the lives of those around us.

It will be seen that these *True Ghost Stories* are not sent out into the world as propaganda for one religion more than another.

They may do something towards making men and women realise the mysteries of life by which we are surrounded; they may help to stem the flood of materialism that is sapping the foundations of civilisation, but if they should only cause one heart-sore man or woman to take hope, and realise how close they may be to that loved one who left behind a void that nothing can fill, then *True Ghost Stories* will, I hope, have fulfilled some purpose.

" CHEIRO."

The name " Cheiro " is derived from the Greek root *Cheir—the hand,* and is pronounced as if written Ki-ro.

PART I

GHOSTS THAT COME UNBIDDEN

" There are more things in heaven and earth, Horatio,
    Than are dreamt of in your philosophy."

SHAKESPEARE : *Hamlet*, Act I.

Psychic phenomena have been investigated and proved by such men as Sir Oliver Lodge, Sir William Crookes, Sir William Barrett, Cæsar Lombroso of Rome, Professor Hyslop of Columbia College, Flammarion of Paris, Professor James of Harvard University, Lord Balfour, Sir Edward Marshall Hall, K.C., Sir Arthur Conan Doyle, the celebrated author of " Sherlock Holmes," etc. etc.

CHAPTER I

THE HAUNTED ENGINE DRIVER AND
A PHANTOM HAND

IN the following story I am compelled for obvious reasons to suppress the name of the great Railway Company in England on whose line the weird occurrence I am about to relate took place.

One evening in the late Autumn, some few years ago, I was sitting reading in my rooms in London, at about ten o'clock, when the street door bell rang, and in a few moments the servant ushered a stranger into my presence.

"Excuse my coming at this hour, sir," he said, "but I am in great trouble and you are the only man in London whom I believe can help me, if you will only listen to my story."

"I am always willing to help anyone in trouble, if it is in my power to do so," I answered. "Take a chair here, near the fire, and I will listen to anything you have to say."

My visitor was a well-built, powerful-looking man. He had a clear-cut, intelligent-looking face, with eyes that looked frank and honest, the type of man that one would select for some position of responsibility.

In the depth of his dark-grey, practical-looking eyes there was, however, a haunted expression, something like one might expect to see in those of some faithful dog that had been frightened and did not know which way to turn for help.

There was something about the man that aroused all my sympathy and at the same time a feeling of intense pity.

He dropped into the chair I had placed for him, without speaking, and just looked at me with an appealing expression in his eyes that I will never forget as long as I live.

Again, I repeated I would listen to anything he had to say and help him if it were in my power to do so.

" Thank you, sir," he said, " but—but—I am afraid you will put me down as a madman when you have heard what I have to tell you."

"No such thing, my good man," I laughed, "I have heard all kinds of things in my strange career, go ahead, and tell me exactly what is troubling you, and you may depend on my doing anything I can to help you."

" Well, first, sir, take a look at my papers, perhaps then you won't think that I have come out of a lunatic asylum."

I glanced at some papers he pushed before me. One was a first class certificate from a school of engineering, the other from a well-known railway Company in the north, recommending him to a similar company saying they had known James Brierly since he had entered their service as an apprentice in their machine shops, and that they considered him the most reliable engine-driver on their staff.

"Since then, sir," he nodded, "I have been up here in London, first on the 'locals,' then on the 'non-stops to the Midlands,' and in the last few months I have been promoted to the biggest engine in the company's service."

"There is certainly nothing of the madman about all that," I smiled.

"Well, no sir," he added gloomily, "but you haven't yet heard my story."

Then making what appeared to be a great effort over himself, he looked me straight in the eyes and said abruptly—

"Do you believe that the dead can return?"

For a moment I was taken off my guard—this was about the last question in the world that one would have expected to issue from the lips of such a man.

He was not the type, however, that one could prevaricate with, besides why should I—still I had no means of knowing what effect my answer would produce—the only thing I always found in difficult conditions, was, to tell the truth and abide by whatever the result might be.

Looking back straight into his eyes, I said, speaking slowly and decidedly :

" I do not know why you should come here to ask such a question, but I will give you my opinion for whatever it is worth. I do believe the so-called dead can return *and do return under certain conditions*. I have had many personal experiences that prove the truth of my words."

The effect was magical—my visitor gripped my hand, and nearly crushed it in his grasp.

" Then I am not mad," he gasped, " Thank God, I have found someone to whom I can speak."

It was indeed a strange story he laid before me, one that even I, with all my experience of occult matters, found difficult to believe.

I will give it as I heard it. I will give it as nearly as possible in the man's own words, the sequel with the everlasting question— why ? the reader can later on answer for himself.

Leaning forward, for a moment he poked up the fire till the bright flames soared up the chimney. For a few seconds, in memory, he had gone back to the far gone days when he got his first fireman's job on a shunter's engine up North.

" Yes, sir " (he seemed to answer my thoughts), " it would have been better for me if I had remained up there and been contented on thirty bob a week, but ' the call of London ' came to me as it comes sooner or later to many a better man.

" We came down, the missus and me, and the baby girl, the only one we ever had ; we took rooms close to the Railway Yards, and for a time I was the happiest man in London.

" My only pal was Jim Robson, he also came from up North, and when Jim found that I was in the same yard, he pushed me on from one job to another until I became his fireman on the Midnight Express, and from that I was soon made driver on one of the ' locals.'

" Then Jim got married—he insisted on my being his ' best man.' God help me when I look back and think of the mockery of it all.

" I thought I loved my wife—she was good to me—as good as ever a woman was to a man.

" What happened I do not know. Jim brought his wife often to see us. One evening when he had to go back to his post on the Midnight Express he told me I was to see her home.

" Jim had bought a little cottage on the main line near a station where my ' local ' made its first stop. Jim told me to take his wife on the train, as I would have just enough time to see her to her door.

" I was proud as any man could be. I saw Jim's wife to her door ; I told her how much

I owed to Jim, and we both agreed that he was the best chap on earth. And so things went on. Everytime my 'local' stopped at that station I used to slip across and have a chat with Jim's wife, and it became a kind of habit month after month, until Jim's little girl was born.

"Jim was disappointed that it was not a boy. He wanted to have a son, and so he thought it was his right to have one. He was a queer man with a fixed code of his own about life, morals and religion, but I don't believe that a better man ever stood in shoe-leather.

"He was not a church-goer in any sense of the word. He was just one of God's good men that was born so, and he never altered.

"After the birth of his little girl he began to change towards me. Gossip had reached his ears of my visits to the cottage, people had told him that every time my 'local' stopped at the station, I had stepped across the lane to see his wife.

"It was quite true what was said. From that evening when I first saw Jim's wife home, I could not help myself, I had to see her at every opportunity. At first there was nothing in it, just a few friendly words, and nothing more, except when my 'local' stopped an extra half hour before the last run home.

"Little by little a change spread over my

whole nature. Day after day I found myself leaning out of the cab as the engine came round the bend in the line just to catch a sight of the cottage and to imagine I saw her waving to me from the porch.

"I would not allow myself to think that I was in love with Jim's wife. I believed I would have killed myself before I would do anything dishonourable, but the yearning and the longing for her grew and grew, until in the end it twisted every thought of honour or manhood that I possessed.

"Perhaps you have never been in love, sir, so you cannot understand.

"Before this came to me, sir, I would have killed, like a mad dog, any man I found running after another man's wife, and— *yet such a thing had come to me.*

"At first there was nothing on her side to give me any encouragement. She was just lonely, that was all.

"Jim was home for a few hours three days a week, but he spent all his Sundays with her. As there were no 'locals' running up and down that day, I never saw them together, for after gossip got to Jim's ears he dropped asking the missus and me to go up to the cottage.

"Sundays became a torture to me. I tried hard to be good to my missus and my little girl, and the more I got in love with Jim's wife, the better I was to them. I took them out somewhere every Sunday as a kind of a sop to my better nature, but I could hardly disguise my torment.

" Jim came up to me one evening in the Engine Yard. He looked me straight in the eyes and said :

" ' Brierly, I have heard some talk about my wife and you. You will have to give up the " local " and take another job. If not, then God help you, for sooner or later I'll have my revenge.'

" Before I had time to answer he turned on his heel and strode down the Yard.

" The next morning I asked for a change from the ' local ' and was put on an engine running to the Midlands and back in the same day, but *again on the main line that ran past the cottage.*

" Day by day my torment increased. In the early morning my engine swung round the bend opposite the cottage and rushed past it again at night.

" Love breeds love, they say. It had commenced to bite into her heart as it had devoured mine.

" Every morning in rain or shine her hand waved to me from the porch ; every night a lamp shone in her window to bid me good-night.

" Things went from bad to worse. I commenced to write to her, my thoughts ran riot, my words went wild. I forgot the danger that Jim might find my letters. I forgot everything but that one woman ; every second of my life seemed but a heart beat that had an answering throb in hers.

"It was no use trying to pull myself together—I had gone too far. Separation intensified my torment until life became a living hell. Only those who have loved as I have can know what I mean.

"Then the tragedy came, swift, terrible, and relentless.

"One dark Saturday night I leaned from the cab to catch for a moment the light of her signal lamp. For the first time for months it was not there. I slowed down to pass the treacherous bend; I pulled the whistle as I had done night after night so that she might hear, but no light came. I opened the throttle again, the train rushed forward—like a man in a dream I reached the end of the journey.

"As I jumped from the engine the newsbill of an evening paper caught my eye. In big black letters, it said :

'TRAGEDY IN A COTTAGE

ENGINE DRIVER KILLS HIS WIFE—HIS CHILD—AND HIMSELF.'

*   *   *   *

"The next day I received notice that I had been promoted to—Jim's place on the Midnight Express."

*   *   *   *

" No, sir, I did not funk it—when a man's heart is dead he is nothing more than a machine. I took *his engine* over that same night. As we slowed down to pass the bend, I did not dare look out—for me there was no cottage—there was nothing but blackness, both in my heart and out.

" Automatically, I pulled the whistle. I wondered if she could hear—and then in spite of being a mere machine, I found scalding tears welling into my eyes and rolling down my face.

" They had given me Jim's fireman. I looked round for him. He was in the back of the cab, standing bare-headed, wiping something from his cheeks. We grasped one another's hands—one moment of weakness—he picked up his shovel, and I went back to the throttle.

" Months went by in uneventful monotony. At night we glanced over our shoulders at the lonely cottage, and the morning later swept by it on our return in the early dawn.

" Jim's name never once crossed our lips—the fireman touched his cap as we passed to his memory ; I raised mine to the memory of his wife.

" Then one night, as unexpected as it was sudden, a strange thing happened, and now, sir, this is where I don't want you to think that the strain on my nerves has driven me mad.

" It was the fireman who noticed it first.

Nearing the bend, I had done as the regulations stated, pulled back the lever to quarter speed, and as we slowed down to make the turn I leaned out of the cab to look at the cottage just as I had always done day after day.

" Suddenly the fireman's voice called me back to myself. With eyes staring out of his head he was pointing to the lever.

" For a second I did not take in what was happening. It was the quickening throb of the engine that made me realise something was wrong. *The lever was being pulled slowly open*—it had already reached the half-speed mark.

" In a flash I had gripped it—forced it back to the quarter mark, and with clenched teeth held it there—*in spite of something that seemed to pull against me.*

" It was almost too late. We were rounding the bend at too much speed, the engine swayed from side to side, the wheels shrieked as they ground against the rails. For a moment I thought we would plunge over the bank, but the dangerous section was passed, the engine straightened itself out and we were safe.

" ' My God! ' the fireman said, as he wiped the sweat from his face, ' that was Jim's hand on the lever—I *know* it was.'

"From that out I took precautions never to take my hand from the lever when coming near the bend—but whether you believe me or not, sir, I have to say that many a time I have felt the pull against me, and a few nights ago *it was stronger than ever.*"

* * * *

He had finished his story, it had done him good to talk it over with someone. His eyes had lost that wistful haunted look they had when he first came in.

But what can he want me to do ? I mentally asked.

Before I could form a question he went on :

" What I want you to do, sir, is this. I want you to come up with me to the Terminus to-night. I want you to talk to my fireman, to tell him my story is all nonsense, something caused by our overwrought nerves. He knows I am taking my missus and the little girl on the train with me to-night. Yes, sir, we are leaving London for good; it has never been lucky for me, sir. I wish I had never seen it. I have got a little cottage up North at the end of the line where I feel sure my missus will be more happy.

" I promised my fireman I would come and tell you the whole thing before we took the train out to-night. We have just got an hour to get to the station. Please, sir, do come with me."

There was such a pleading tone in his voice and in his eyes that I had not the heart to refuse. What good my going to see his fireman would do, I could not imagine, yet I felt I had to do it.

Finding a cab in the street we reached the Terminus about half an hour before he took his train out.

In an empty carriage next the engine his wife and child were already seated, with all their luggage round them. The wife appeared to be an exceptionally nice kind of woman, with a peculiarly sad expression of resignation in her eyes. The little girl was a dear little thing, about five or six years of age; she was playing with a baby doll in her lap and caressing it with all the tenderness of a mother.

A boy passed with chocolates, I bought her a box and to thank me she held up her little face to be kissed.

Standing at the steps of the engine was the fireman—one of those square-jawed well-set-up young fellows that are the backbone of England's working-class.

He took my outstretched hand in that shy diffident kind of way that men of his type so often have when meeting a stranger for the first time.

Brierly left us to go on his engine and the fireman and I walked a few yards up the platform.

"I'm glad you saw him, sir," he said. "I'm sure you did him some good."

For a moment I hardly knew what to say.

"It may have done him good to tell someone his queer story," I answered, "but I don't know that I was able to help him in any way."

" No, sir, neither you nor anyone else can do much, I fear. I just persuaded him to go as I felt he had to talk to someone to relieve his mind, but mark my words, sir," he added, " the worst has yet to come."

Much use, I mentally thought, of my telling a man like this that the whole thing was nonsense.

" Have you really seen the lever move ? " I asked, looking him straight in the eyes.

" Seen it move ? My God ! I've not only seen it move, but *I've felt it move,* and what's more, sir, each time lately that it occurs, the pull has got stronger and stronger. I suppose Brierly did not tell you that only three nights ago he had to yell to me for help, and we both had to hold the lever back with all our strength, or the engine would have dashed at sixty miles an hour round the bend, and neither he nor I would be here to tell the tale."

" Did you *see* anything ? " I asked.

He looked me straight in the eyes.

" As plain as I see you here to-night, sir, I saw the shape of my old mate Jim standing by Brierly's side, and what's more, *with his right hand gripping the lever, as I've seen him do a hundred times in his life.*"

" Could it not be that your nerves have got overwrought and you imagined it ? " I said, as calmly as I could.

The next moment I felt sorry I had asked such a question.

The big strong man at my side looked at

me with contempt—" Do I look like a man who sees ghosts ? " he laughed grimly.

We had reached the end of our walk, we had turned and were looking back at the train; people were crowding in to take their seats, some laughing and joking as they said good-bye, some clasping some loved one in their arms. Mail bags were being thrown in, luggage being hurried up, the usual bustle and last-minute rush of a long train starting for the North.

" Some nights," the fireman went on, " I shiver when I see the passengers loading up. It nearly paralyses me to think what would happen *if the lever got pulled right over* and the engine plunged at sixty miles an hour round the bend."

" Have you never thought of speaking to the Directors of the Railway ? " I asked.

Again the big man looked at me with contempt.

" Do you take me for a damned fool, or a half-witted idiot—a common fireman daring to speak to one of the money-gods that control this Company. My God, sir, I don't want to be packed off to a lunatic asylum, and that's exactly what would happen. We daren't even address one of them except through our union. There's the first whistle, sir, I must be off."

Brierly's wife was leaning out of the carriage window. It was the end coach nearest the engine, it was the only one that had no passengers in it. Brierly, I thought, had evidently chosen it, so as to have the wife and child *as near to him as possible.*

Another whistle—Brierly's wife lifted up the little girl for him to kiss, she put her tiny face up to him and her arms round his neck; he broke away, then turned and kissed her again and again.

Another second and he was back on his engine. Leaning over the side he gripped my hand.

" Thank you, sir," he said. " Thank you for coming to bid us good-bye."

A third whistle—Brierly's hand was already on the lever—a hiss of steam, then another and another—the monster of steel quivered with life—wheels turned faster and faster, a wave of a hand—and the long train rushed forward into the night.

I was the last to leave the platform— something in me, I knew not what, seemed to have gone with those men on the engine, and followed them out into the night. A presentiment of horror and tragedy gripped my very soul.

And yet what could I do ? We mortals are worse than helpless when Fate takes the helm of things into its own hands.

I walked all the way back to my rooms. I thought the night air would steady my nerves.

The fire was still burning in my sitting-room. I threw myself into the chair I had been sitting in, when only a few hours before Brierly was with me telling his story.

Two hours went by. Suddenly the telephone bell rang. Who could want me at such a time in the early morning, I wondered.

A voice at the other end said:

" Is your name ' Cheiro ? ' I have a message from a man who has been through a smash-up on the railway. He wants me to tell you the Midnight Express met with an accident at ' the bend.' The engine and first carriage jumped the track, Jim Brierly, his wife and child were killed, the fireman was thrown off and wants you to come to the Railway Hospital at once."

CHAPTER II

A SPIRIT BRINGS A PRIEST TO GIVE ABSOLUTION TO A DYING MAN

ONE evening after dinner in my house in the South of England, the Parish Priest, Father Jackson, dropped in to have a chat.

Father Jackson was an interesting study of humanity. He was loved by everyone —Roman Catholic, Protestant, or heathen (and there were a few of the latter in that quiet little village)—all had a good word to say of the " Father," as he was affectionately called.

He was devoted to his church : it had been, when he first came to the Parish, a poor little wooden shanty with the rain coming through its iron roof, and a congregation consisting of a dozen " souls " so old, and crippled with rheumatism, that once they got on their knees they generally remained there until Mass was over.

In ten years he had rebuilt the little church, but even brick was not good enough for him : it had to be done with Portland stone ; his congregation had increased to over two hundred, including many of the " heathen," and people came long distances to hear him preach.

When not on the subject of religion he was the broadest minded man I have ever met. He loved everything that was out of the ordinary and was extremely well read on all scientific problems of the day.

He and I had many discussions on occult subjects of various kinds, and although he would always preface his arguments by insisting that " the Church " did not countenance such things, yet he was the very man who, in the end, related to me one of the most striking stories of the human side of ghostly manifestation that I have ever heard.

On the evening in question we had been discussing some of the strange and inexplicable things that had happened recently in my house, and one incident in particular had strongly appealed to him in which a spirit had insisted on a certain work being carried out which had brought benefit and great happiness to all concerned.

To my surprise, instead of arguing against this subject as he generally did, he leaned back in his chair and told me the following :

" I am inclined to admit," he began, " that the dead may return under some exceptional circumstances, to do some good work for example ; then perhaps they may be allowed to revisit the earth. An experience of this kind has happened in my own life.

" I was once an assistant Priest in a very

poor parish in Glasgow—the kind of place that young priests are sent to, so as to get them thoroughly well 'broken in.' I had lodgings with another priest—a man twice my age, who was so infirm that I did the greater part of his work as well as my own.

"One night I got home more tired out than usual. I took off my wet boots, put them to dry by the side of the fire while my companion poured out a bowl of soup, that he had been keeping hot for me for hours. I was tired out mentally and physically : there had been for months an epidemic of sickness in Glasgow, a cold hard winter as well, and what with sick calls, people dying, and the regular work of a Priest, I was completely worn out.

"With a sigh of relief I stretched myself out in an easy chair before the fire. Outside the wind howled, and the rain pattered against the window. 'Thank God!' I thought, 'I have no more sick calls to-night.'"

*   *   *   *

"A faint knock at the outside door. I pretended I did not hear it. My companion threw me over the evening paper—he also looked as if he had heard nothing. A minute or so went past—*the knock came again.*

"I commenced to read the paper out loud : 'Storm raging in the North of Scotland—Telegraph wires down—Floods on the Clyde.' *The knock came again—a queer persistent kind of knock.* I threw down the paper, got up and opened the door. There was nobody there, nothing but blank darkness. I waited a moment but no one appeared. I closed the door and went back to the fire.

" ' It's only the wind,' my companion said. ' No one would want to call you out on such a night, except, of course, some person was dying.'

" *The knock came again.* We waited without speaking—again, and this time very much louder. I threw the door open. In the flickering light from the gas lamp across the street the figure of a man stood as if waiting for me.

" I can see the man's face in my mind now. A rough-looking individual with a handkerchief tied round his throat, a distinct Irish type, a determined expression on his face and a pair of eyes with a weird longing look that I shall never forget.

" He did not speak, he just beckoned me to come.

" 'All right,' I answered, 'wait a moment, and I'll be with you.'

" With difficulty I pulled on my wet boots and my wet coat, and taking what Priests carry with them for emergencies I turned back to the door.

" The man gave me a sign to follow him, and started off at a pace I found difficult to keep up with.

" I thought I knew that part of Glasgow well, but the man leading me seemed to know it better. He turned down one side street after another, and if I was a little behind he waited for me and then started off again.

" ' He evidently believes someone has not long to live,' I thought, and I pushed on as fast as I could through the driving rain.

" We had reached the docks and had turned up a side street where there was a block of tenement houses—a horrible rabbit warren, with each room let out separately.

" At a stone staircase at the farthest end of the block I could see the man waiting for me. We went up the stairs almost together, he keeping only a few steps ahead. Up, up we went, till we reached the last room on the top floor. The door was open, the light of an oil lamp shone out in the passage. The man entered, passed up to the head of the bed. I could see him stoop and grasp the dying man's hand, the next moment he was gone.

" I looked round; there was no door but the one I was coming in by, and yet the individual had disappeared.

" The dying man had already seen me. 'Oh, Father,' he gasped, ' you have come at last. Pat Egan told me he would fetch a Priest and he kept his word.'

" ' Where is Pat Egan ? ' I asked.

" ' He died in Australia twenty years ago. But, Father, listen to me. Don't mind that, you will understand when you hear my story.

" ' Pat Egan and I met in the bush some four hundred miles on the other side of Melbourne. We were both of us outcasts from our fellow men, outcasts who, perhaps, never had a chance to do better or to know better. As the saying is, our hand was against every man's and every man's hand was against us.

" ' There was a price set on our heads ; we kept as far from towns or civilisation as we could. Between us was a blood pact sealed by the dangers we had passed through together.

" ' I never knew much about religion. The only time I heard of Christ was when I was in gaol, and in those days religion and " skilly " did not seem to suit me.

" ' Pat Egan, on the contrary, was a Catholic. He carried a cross his mother gave him next his heart, he said his prayers every night, whether his bed was a hole in a rock or a hollow in the sand.

" ' One night the fever came. Egan got it worse than me. Our strength was burned up, and, from being two strong men who feared nothing, we became weak as infants deserted by their mother. The fever seized Egan worse than it did me. At last I realised that the end was not far off, and, ill as I was myself, I sat day and night bathing his poor head and trying to soothe him to sleep.

" ' We were on the fringe of the desert, far

from the haunts of men, two poor lost out-
laws fighting for life as we had always fought,
clinging to life as we had always clung ; but
to one of us Death had already laid his
claim.

" ' Egan's hand had gripped mine. " Mate,"
he said, " do one thing for me, and *when it
comes your turn to die I will do the same for
you.*"

" ' I bent nearer to him—his eyes burned
into mine—he knew he was about to ask
what was next to the impossible. " *Fetch a
Priest,*" he said faintly.'

*   *   *   *

" ' When morning came I was half way
to the nearest town. Illness, fatigue, hunger,
are idle words when the Will takes command.
Night came again. In the distance I saw a
spire with a Cross—the Cross of that Christ
I had only heard of when in gaol.

" ' I told my story to a Priest.

" ' Back through the night two horses
galloped down the long white trail. Then the
trail was left, and the tractless wild began.
On, on, and on, till the dawn came and the
smoke of the fire I had left rose in the distance
and beckoned us to hurry. It was the signal
that Egan still lived. I had placed faggots
within his reach to keep the fire going.

" ' The priest arrived in time. Egan had
the consolation he had asked. Far from men,

on the fringe of the desert, the prodigal had been received back.

"'The dying hand gripped mine. The lips were moving. "Mate," he whispered, "*when your turn comes I will do the same for you.*"'"

CHAPTER III

THE HAUNTING HORROR OF THE WHITE BAT

CAN THE DEAD CAST A SPELL OF VENGEANCE UPON THE LIVING?
THE SANCTUARY OF SEPULCHRE WAS PART OF THE RELIGION OF THE
ANCIENT EGYPTIANS. VIOLATION MEANT SOMETHING WORSE THAN
DEATH. BY POTENT SPELLS, THAT CAN ONLY BE UNDERSTOOD BY THE
LORE OF OCCULTISM, THEY GUARDED THEIR TOMBS BY THREATS
DIRECTED AGAINST ANY WHO SHOULD DISTURB THEIR RESTING-PLACE.
IN THIS STORY I RELATE HOW I WAS SOUGHT OUT BY A DISTRACTED
MAN WHO HAD INCURRED THE VENGEANCE OF THE MIGHTY DEAD;
AND HOW I MYSELF WAS DRAWN INTO THE CIRCLE OF THE SPELL;
UNTIL FINALLY IT REACHED ITS CLIMAX UNDER CIRCUMSTANCES OF
MYSTERY AND HORROR.

THE Uncanny has its abiding fascination for all people. The unusual and strange that seems indeed supernatural, that is, above natural understanding, has in all ages been regarded with shuddering wonder. And while the old Seers and Wise Men were able by their knowledge of Occult laws to fathom many a seeming mystery, they were in consequence regarded as dangerous persons who had associated themselves with the Evil One.

I can write with perfect truth that I have had experiences of the Uncanny that defy the laws of Reason. Many of them have been

through association with those who have
come to my consulting-rooms, shadowed by
some strange Fate or burdened by an in-
stinctive premonition of calamity. In some
instances I have been able to help : in others
I, too, have been drawn into the circle of the
Supernatural. In London, Paris, Egypt,
India, China and elsewhere, I have been at
various times at grips with the Uncanny. I
propose to set down these experiences as
simply as possible, explaining, where I am
able to understand, the various forces and
laws that in my judgment have brought
about these mysterious happenings.

" Cheiro, can the dead cast a spell of vengeance upon the Living ? "

Thus, one afternoon in my rooms in London, this question was whispered to me by the
haggard lips of a caller who had presented
himself with a letter from the late Mr. W. T.
Stead, whose interest in the Occult had been
cut short by his untimely death by drowning
through the loss of the *Titanic*.

My caller explained that in January, 1912,
three months before the disaster to the great
ship, he had been in London and had called
upon Mr. Stead. The conversation had
turned upon the subject of death-warnings,
and particularly on the old Egyptian spells
used to guard the sanctity of tombs. Mr.
Stead had then remarked on several striking
cases he personally knew, where mummies
had brought a train of disaster upon those

removing them from their tombs; he went on to advise his friend to see myself, kindly saying it was a subject I knew far more about than he did.

Mr. Hendry, my caller, was, as he told me, a wealthy Irish-American who had made a fortune in New York on the Stock Exchange. He had retired and married late in life, and had gone to Egypt owing to his interest in tomb excavations. Thus, there had been set in motion a train of circumstances bringing death and disaster, and incidentally ultimately involving me as well.

Mr. Hendry was an elderly man of cultured appearance. I sensed he was labouring under some deep emotion or suppressed fear. As always was my habit, I tried to put myself into a sympathetic frame of mind, asking no questions, knowing from experience that my visitor had come to ask me questions and get my advice.

The words " Cheiro, can the Dead Cast a Spell of Vengeance over the Living ? " were uttered while he fumbled at a small parcel he held in his hand. Unwrapping it, he laid upon my table an object I immediately recognised as an Egyptian scarab.

" Cheiro," he said, " can you tell me anything concerning this antiquity ? "

Now, as it happens, I have had a close association with the land of the Pharaohs, and have, moreover, been privileged to be tutored in much of the mystic lore of the

Egyptians by a student of such things whom I met in Cairo in former days. I therefore said, after minutely inspecting the scarab :

"From its general appearance I should say it has been taken from a tomb where it was used as a seal upon the final wrapping of a mummy, closing the ends of the covering at the breast. As it is shaped like a bat, I assume it was found in a tomb of the time of Cheops of the Fourth Dynasty ; for in his reign this king was deified as a Bat."

Mr. Hendry seemed very interested by what I had said. As I laid the scarab down he said in a low, intense voice :

"Cheiro, I am under a curse—a spell, call it what you will. It has robbed me of the dearest woman in the world, sent my schemes crashing to ruin, brought my best friend to suicide, and now I fear its malignance aims at my own life. I want you to tell me what the Future has in store for me. Be frank, for God knows, after all I have endured, anything is better than this torturing suspense."

As he finished speaking I was surprised to notice his forehead was damp with perspiration.

"Supposing," I said gently, "you tell me a little about this trouble, then perhaps I shall be able to help you." It was then he unfolded one of the strangest tales I have ever heard in my consulting-rooms.

He told me he had been staying the previous year at Shepheard's Hotel, Cairo, and while there had heard of some remarkable new excavations in the Valley of the Kings. Investigating, he found the work stopped through the death of a German archæologist, who had died suddenly. A strange fear had seized the native workers; they were positive the larger tomb, of which the outer chamber only had been reached, was haunted by evil spirits who had caused the death of the German.

However, Mr. Hendry was a resolute man and he determined to take over the work, obtaining a permit for the purpose. By bribery he got some more natives, and eventually three chambers were laid bare, leading in the end to a sarcophagus containing Royal remains; as the door bore the seal of Cheops IV.

Finally, the chamber was breached and the temporary installation of electric light revealed a wonderful golden coffin. Working alone, for none of the natives would enter, Hendry raised the lid and the secret of the ages was revealed. The mummy was that of an ancient priest, perfect even to his long white beard, and obviously of the Royal College of Mystic Priests founded by Cheops in honour of his deification.

" Cheiro," said Mr. Hendry impressively, when he had reached this part in his absorbing narrative, " on the breast of the mummy was this scarab. As I touched it to tear it away, it seemed as though a horror of fear descended upon me like a cloud. The electric lights dimmed to a faint glimmer; a cold sighing wind filled the cave; and I heard fluttering shapes passing through the air and brushing my face. *I judged them to be bats.*

"I confess that a panic seized me. With the scarab in my hand I stumbled from the chamber, panting, and only longing for the outer air. After I rallied my nerves I determined to go back to complete my work. But I was tired and faint, and eventually decided to wait till the next day.

"When I got to my hotel my wife received me with a scared face. She was always averse to my digging and delving among the tombs. During the afternoon she had been a prey to nervous fears for my safety. I promised that I would not go to the tomb again.

"To rid my mind of disturbing impressions, my wife and I went for an excursion down the Nile as far as Luxor. Camping on the South Bank I quickly became normal again. The scarab I found I kept carefully concealed and did not speak about it to any of my acquaintances."

Then in a lower voice, and with the tears filling his eyes, Mr. Hendry went on to tell how one night he was awakened by an unusual sound. Gradually he was aware that *a snow-white bat was flitting ceaselessly round the tent.*

"I peered through the flap and I cannot tell you with what horror I saw the ghastly visitant of the night circling the tent and occasionally emitting a squeaking note. I drove it away; I fell asleep again, but my dreams were of tombs and filled with vague horrors."

Mr. Hendry went on to tell how his wife grew melancholy and fearful of something she could not express. One morning he awoke to find her dead. The cause was a complete mystery. The doctors could only say it was heart failure through some shock.

After this, disaster after disaster had fallen upon my visitor. His investments turned out badly; a trusted friend committed suicide in New York after confessing he had embezzled forty thousand dollars of money entrusted to him. His father, resident in New Orleans, suddenly sickened and passed away. And, finally, the bereaved widower found himself alone in life and *haunted by the snow-white bat.*

" Cheiro," he cried, " is it insanity, or something so devilish that it is beyond human understanding ? I have heard, of course, that a curse rests upon those who rifle the tombs of the Egyptian dead. I have laughed at it as an old wives' tale. But now——" and he shuddered violently.

Growing calmer, he said that often he had a frightful nightmare of a giant bat resting upon him and gradually suffocating the life out of him. "I dread to sleep," he said. "And I want to know how this is all going to end."

I got him to write down his birth-date and at the same time examined his hand. I could see that a tragic end was in store for him. But in his distracted condition I did not think it advisable to tell him all the truth. I soothed and heartened him until he grew more composed. The subject of his length of days seemed to have passed from his mind, and he did not refer to it again.

Just before leaving he suddenly said :

" Cheiro, will you do me a favour ? I am called away for several days on business. May I leave in your charge—THIS ? " He placed in my hands the bat-shaped scarab.

I must confess that, as my hand came in contact with it, a strangely apprehensive thrill ran through me. I was professionally keen to find out more, if possible, of this relic of the dead, but underneath this a cold feeling of fear seemed to possess me. My caller watched me keenly.

" You are not afraid, Cheiro ? " he asked.

" No," I said impulsively. " I will keep it in my possession until you come to claim it."

A few days later I went for a short recreation to a house I had taken for the summer in the island of Jersey. That night when I went to bed I placed the scarab on a small table by my bed.

Sleep came quickly. But then came dreams—strange, haunted dreams with an Egyptian setting. I was in great halls with solemn colossal figures carved on monuments of stone. The scene changed, and I was passing through endless corridors that ran downwards into the earth. At last I stood in a small chamber, which grew smaller, while suffocation gripped my throat. I was choking, dying, unable to move, buried alive! With a strangled cry, I awoke to find myself bathed in perspiration, with a horrible feeling that something was clutching at my throat.

The large window in the room was facing the foot of my bed. It was a night of brilliant moonlight; the blind had been left undrawn. As I gazed at the window, trying to collect my confused recollections, I experienced a thrill of horror. For there, pressed against the window pane, staring through with brilliant eyes that seemed fixed upon me with menacing intentness, *was a huge white bat.* The loathly nocturnal creature remained motionless, its pointed ears erect, waiting and watching as if it sought human prey.

Then suddenly it was gone. The spell broken, I leapt from the bed. Far away, over the tree tops, ghostly in the moonlight, I could see it floating upon swift wings.

The next day I found my throat stiff and swollen. I called in a doctor and he was frankly puzzled. All he could suggest was some bite, perhaps a poisonous insect. I held my counsel.

On returning to London, Mr. Hendry called upon me for the scarab. I must confess I gladly gave it up. He asked, curiously, if I

had noticed anything queer about it. Something sealed my lips, except that I begged
him to take it back to Egypt and leave it in
the place where he had found it.

A look of fatalistic obstinacy crossed his
face. He wrung my hand, and left me without
a word.

In my inner conviction I felt the spell had
gripped him and that he was treading the
road that must lead to tragedy.

But Fate tarried. The incident of the
scarab had almost faded from my mind when,
in an idle moment, I took up a copy of the
Paris edition of the *New York Herald*, a
newspaper I invariably scanned. My eye
caught a paragraph : " Mysterious death of
an American Visitor," and detailed the tragic
passing of Mr. Hendry, who had been found
dead in bed in a hotel in the Rue la Fayette.
From inquiries I made, it appears that a
visitor in an adjoining room heard one " long
thrilling scream " in the night ; hearing no
other sound, he had fallen asleep again. It
was recalled that the dead man had insisted
upon having the shutters fastened over his
bedroom window ; when he was found dead,
the shutters were thrown back, while the top
window was lowered. All that the doctors
could say was " death from syncope "—
or failure of the heart from some unknown
cause. The scarab was not included in the
official inventory of the dead man's effects.
It had vanished.

Reason may laugh at spells woven by those who have been dead thousands of years. But it is a significant fact that those who disturb Egyptian dead are rarely safe from disaster, if not death. Egypt to-day is full of turmoil and unrest ; and those who still cherish the ancient wisdom, say, the occult influences set in motion by the priests who were the sacred guardians of the Pharaohs, are potent to avenge those who desecrate their tombs.

" *I am fully convinced that the soul is indestructible, and its activity will continue through eternity.*"

J. VON GOËTHE.

CHAPTER IV

THE FAMOUS MUMMY CASE OF THE BRITISH MUSEUM

MR. DOUGLAS MURRAY, a well-known man in London, came into my rooms one afternoon. I had at that time not the slightest idea who my visitor was, but even if I had, it would have made no difference to the strange story I am about to relate.

To my mind, my visitor was just one of the many men " about town " who came to consult me out of curiosity or otherwise.

At that moment my visitor had no particular interest or pursuit in life. He was like so many other rich young men who went about " killing time " as pleasantly as possible, till they in the natural course of events would themselves be killed by it.

Laughingly he placed himself in the chair opposite to me and, putting his hands on the small table between us, said in a joking way :

" Which of my hands are you going to take ? "

A strange feeling I cannot describe came over me. I was what might be called " a trained sensitive " with long years of experience behind me. This being so, I was generally able to mask my emotions and prevent an expression of one kind or another making itself manifest in my face.

In this case, however, *as I took my visitor's right hand* in my own, an unaccountable feeling of dread and horror seemed to creep from it, and as quickly as I took it, I dropped it back on the cushion.

" What on earth is wrong with my right hand ? " my visitor laughed.

Then it was that the hand itself *seemed to speak to me*. It was not that I attempted to read it, there was no need for me to make such an effort. It was as if my sensitive soul was taken possession of by some occult force of which I cannot give any explanation, but which at many times in my life has appeared to overwhelm me and forced me to visualise the future of my clients in a series of pictures one after the other.

Without giving any regard to the effect my words might make, and with the feeling of listening to myself speaking without the power of preventing the words coming from my lips, I blurted out rapidly :

" I feel this right hand of yours *will not be yours for long*. A picture forms in my mind of a gun of some kind bursting and shattering it to pieces. This is followed by terrible suffering and finally the entire arm will have to be amputated," and I added quickly : " Your hand, sir, seems to be calling to me to try and save it from this impending disaster."

Of course my visitor laughed. Is there any man who would not laugh under such circumstances?

"Your hand shows me another picture," I went on. "It draws a number out of a lottery, the number gives a prize that you do not want to have. Out of obstinacy and fatalism you take it, and from that moment out commences a series of misfortunes, beginning with the loss of your right arm and leading up to your own death."

"But, Cheiro," my visitor laughed, "have you ever heard of a man who, if he is lucky enough to draw a prize, is not only too glad to take what he wins? As for me, I have never won a thing in a lottery yet, and I don't believe I ever shall. But does this wonderful hand of mine tell you what this extraordinary prize is likely to be?"

In spite of his cheerful banter, another picture formed clearly and distinctly in my mind. At first it took only the shape of an oblong object that looked decidedly like a coffin. Suddenly strange hieroglyphics appeared, and it stood out as an Egyptian sarcophagus with a carved figure on the lid.

"Don't touch it," I could hear myself saying, "I beg of you don't touch it; if you do, it will bring misfortune to you and all others who have anything to do with it."

"My dear Cheiro," my visitor laughed,

" if you work yourself into a state like this with all your clients, it is I who must predict that before long, it is you who will be in an oblong box with your name on a brass plate in good old English lettering."

We both laughed, but before he left he handed me his card " so as to remember his name," he said.

A few years later Mr. Douglas Murray visited me again. The *sleeve of his right arm was empty* and fastened across the front of his coat. He was looking pale and haggard, the shadow of his former self.

" Well, it all happened exactly as you foresaw, Cheiro," he said.

He then told me the following :

He had been to Egypt—went there out of a sudden whim to do some shooting with two friends who were going up the Nile.

Before he left Cairo his dragoman brought him to see a mummy case in an unusually good state of preservation. The hieroglyphics on it described its ancient owner to have been a High-Priestess of the famous Temple of Amen-Ra. The outside of the case bore her image worked out in enamel and gold.

Although he felt, he told me, an extraordinary aversion to having anything to do with this mummy case, he could not resist the temptation to buy it, which in the end he did, and had it sent to his hotel.

That night, as his friends seemed jealous of his wonderful find, he suggested they should draw lots for it—*he drew the winning number*.

Someone suggested that, as there were three in the party, it should be drawn for three times and the man who won it twice should be declared the owner. Douglas Murray drew the winning number for *the first, second and third time*.

That night he gave orders for the mummy case to be packed and sent to his address in London.

A few days later, when shooting up the Nile, the gun he was carrying exploded in his right hand. Suffering the most intense agony, he ordered the Dahabeeah to be returned to Cairo; a headwind of unusual force prevented the boat making much headway, and it was upwards of ten days before he reached his hotel.

By this time gangrene had set in. The doctors did their utmost to prevent it spreading, but in spite of everything that science could do, after weeks of suffering, the right arm had to be cut off above the elbow.

On the voyage back to England both his companions died and were buried at sea. By a singular fate two trunks which contained various valuable scarabs and curiosities he had purchased in Egypt were stolen on the ship's arrival at Tilbury, and in spite of the very large reward he offered, were never recovered or heard of again.

Feeling extremely ill and in a very depressed state of mind, he reached home to find the mummy case had already been unpacked and was waiting for him in the hall.

"You may not believe me, Cheiro," he said, "but if such a thing could be, as I looked at the carved face of the Priestess on the outside of the mummy case, her eyes seemed to come to life, and I saw such a look of hate in them that my very blood seemed to turn to ice."

The following day a well-known literary woman called to interview him on his return. She heard the story, laughed at it, told him nothing occult could affect her, and persuaded him to let her take the mummy case to her house in the outskirts of London.

From the moment the case passed inside her door, misfortune after misfortune followed. Her mother, coming down the stairs to welcome her, fell, broke her thigh, and after months of suffering, died. The man she was engaged to, for no apparent reason, backed out of his engagement and refused to marry her. Within a few months every living pet—and she had three or four prize dogs—went mad and had to be destroyed.

Finally, she became ill herself with a peculiar wasting illness that could not be explained, and at last, becoming terrified with the many misfortunes that had so suddenly appeared, she telephoned her lawyer to come out to prepare her will.

The hard-headed practical man of law, without even asking her permission, had the mummy case that night returned to Douglas Murray.

Having made up his mind to rid himself completely of the thing that had brought him so much suffering, and being determined not to allow any of his friends to own it, he reasoned that the best place to send it would be the Egyptian Section of the British Museum.

Feeling too ill to see about the necessary formalities himself, he called in an old friend to his aid, to make the arrangements.

This man, being an ardent Egyptologist, was only too glad of an opportunity to examine thoroughly the hieroglyphics on the case and, while waiting for the decision of the Council of the British Museum, he had it removed to his own house.

A few weeks later his friends were startled by the news that he was found dead one morning in his bed. At the inquest that followed, his valet testified that from the night the mummy case reached the house, his master had become troubled with insomnia. An empty bottle of chloral was found by his bedside and the verdict was " death by misadventure."

Finally the case was accepted by the British Museum. After a while extraordinary reports reached the ears of the authorities from time to time of strange happenings that took place in the Egyptian Section. It was rumoured that some unaccountable thing happened to anyone who attempted to make any drawing or sketch of this remarkable-looking mummy case.

A well-known artist, a man I knew particularly well, attempted to draw it on no less than four occasions. Each time he met with a bad accident, the last time being run over by a horse and cab as he left the gates of the Museum, and the sketch he was carrying was completely destroyed.

The authorities at the Museum became annoyed at the curiosity the case excited and had it removed to the cellars. Finally, all trace of it disappeared and the rumour went round London that it had been presented to the Egyptian Section of the New York Museum and was actually on the *Titanic* when she went to her doom on her first voyage in April, 1912.

Douglas Murray lived for some years after the case left his possession, but he was never the same after he lost his arm. I saw him on many occasions up to the time of his death a few years ago. His only son, Captain Frank Wyndham Sholto Douglas Murray, died early in the spring of 1928.

CHAPTER V

GHOSTLY HAND WRITES DEATH WARNING FOR MILLIONAIRE ON BEDROOM MIRROR

IN MY MANY EXPERIENCES OF THE UNCANNY THERE ARE FEW THAT COMPARE WITH THE REMARKABLE STORY I WOULD NOW RELATE CONCERNING THE TRAGIC DEATH OF MR. REUBEN BEYFUS, A WEALTHY AMERICAN JEW, WHO WAS A FREQUENT VISITOR TO LONDON AND NOTED FOR HIS GENEROSITY TO THE CHARITIES DESIGNED FOR THE HELP OF HIS POORER BRETHREN

CAN a person be sentenced to death by some premonitory warning, and despite every conceivable effort to avoid its fulfilment, finally die *on the day and the hour foreshadowed*?

My experience has taught me that such cases do occur. In passing I may record that when in the consulting-room I saw evidence in the hands of a client of a sudden death, or a clear indication that such and such a year would mark *Finis* to a career, I was always cautious in revealing such a dread secret unless specifically asked.

I usually found that men who lived the busiest and most useful lives were most anxious to know exactly the sum total of their years, and would then, with methodical care, prepare for a contingency they regarded as inevitable. Fatalism of this kind seemed to give a calm spirit of preparation. On the other hand, I have met many who have longed to know the allotted span of days and yet have obviously shrunk from the truth.

But in thinking over the extraordinary fact that some people have received premonitory warnings of death, there springs at once to my memory the astounding case of Mr. Reuben Beyfus.

This gentleman was head of a famous Jewish family—a wealthy man who was as much at home in London, Paris, Berlin, etc., as in Boston, U.S.A., where he lived. It was in that city I first met him and his charming family.

While visiting Boston during one of my American tours, Mrs. Beyfus called on me for a consultation. She was a handsome woman with a striking personality ; was leader of the musical set in that city, had always had her box for the season at the Opera, and was a particularly kind patron to young singers and struggling artists.

Mrs. Beyfus was one of those few personalities that seem to radiate as it were an " atmosphere " of happiness. She entered my room at the Hotel Brunswick with a smile on her face, and an expression in her eyes as much as to say : " Why do I want to hear what the future holds for me ? I have everything the world can give me."

It had been my custom to train myself not to judge by outward appearances, but to try and get behind the " mask " my visitors so often wore. Yet here I felt there was no concealment. At last I had met a genuinely happy woman.

With a merry laugh she pulled off her gloves and held out both hands. Hers was quite an easy " life " to read. She had been one of " Fate's Favourites " from her early days. Life's stream, so muddy to others, had been to her a river of gold—whatever she had wished for she had got : a good husband and one devoted to her, a boy as handsome as a young god ; a voice, yes, one that few prima donna's could equal. What more could there be to ask for ?

" Up to thirty-five, my age now, you have told me everything exactly ; but why stop, pointing to the end of that line ? Am I going to die ? " she asked.

" No," I said, and perhaps rather abruptly I added : " No, but I think your husband is ; and after that you won't much care what happens."

My client burst into a fit of incredulous laughter.

" Oh! " she cried, " that is too funny! Why, he is as strong as an ox, the very picture of health. You must come and see him."

Before I had recovered my self-possession she had mapped out that I should come to her box at the opera that night, go back to their home for supper with Calvé, Jean de Resky and other singers, and I must " make the acquaintance of my extremely healthy husband, and the best man that God ever gave to a woman."

I found Mr. Beyfus a most charming and interesting man, and we became good friends. Neither she nor I ever mentioned my prediction to him ; in fact, as I viewed his healthy and virile appearance, a doubt as to my forecast troubled my mind.

A month went past, and one evening after dinner we went into his study to see some plans he had prepared for the building of a magnificent block of offices in the centre of Boston.

" How long will all that take ? " Mrs. Beyfus asked.

" Five years," he answered, " before the whole plan is completed, but I will move into my new offices on the street floor in about a year."

" Splendid," she cried. " It will be a monument to you, Reuben. But after the five years, what do you intend to do then ? "

" Well," he said, " I guess by then I will have made enough to retire. We will take a yacht, go round the world and I will realise my heart's desire—to see Jerusalem before I die." He paused and added : " Remember, that must be done, no matter what else may happen."

I left them, happily counting their golden chickens. I felt glad to get away ; I could not explain why. Perhaps my spirit had come in contact with the dread Fate that was even then rapidly approaching them.

I got home, but I could not sleep. The happy, successful face of Mr. Beyfus and the joyous laugh of his wife seemed to haunt me. I seemed to feel that a horrible shadow of gloom was gathering round them.

Morning came. I was already dressed and determined to stretch my legs up Tremont Street and across the Common, but as I reached the street to my amazement I saw the butler from the Beyfus's house rapidly approaching.

" The master wants you to come to him at once, sir," he said in an agitated voice.

" Is Mr. Beyfus ill ? " I asked.

" I don't know what the matter is, sir. He came down to the breakfast-room this morning white as a sheet, and trembling all over."

It was no distance over to Commonwealth Avenue. Mr. and Mrs. Beyfus were waiting in the study. All was confusion ; Mrs. Beyfus was sobbing as if her heart would break.

" My dear friend," Mr. Beyfus began at once. " You are accustomed to queer, supernatural happenings, but can you explain the following :

" Last night you were here. I was laying out plans for the future—you remember the office building, the finest in Boston I was going to build. This morning I had the details of the scheme on the table in my bedroom. I was more enthusiastic than ever about it, and had just taken up the 'phone to make an appointment with the contractors, when *across the mirror of my dressing-table I saw some words slowly appearing.* I confess they froze the blood in my veins. You know I am not superstitious; you know I hate even your study of the hand, and would never let you look at mine. I have a horror of spiritualism and all so-called phenomena. Yet it was *to a man like me that this extraordinary event happened this morning.*"

He paused and passed a hand across his eyes.

"What were the words you saw?" I asked.

His eyes had a strange, frightened look in them as he replied: "Across the top of the mirror appeared the words:

"'*Twelve months from to-day Reuben Beyfus will be gathered to his fathers.*'"

I saw that Mrs. Beyfus remembered my prediction. Stealthily she looked at her palm and then at me.

It was in vain I argued that it was all some delusion. He was a strong healthy man, and should live for years, and so forth.

"No, no," he said, "you only say that to comfort me. I feel in my very bones that the message is for me. On this day twelve months hence, I will be no more. I promised my father that I would see Jerusalem before I died; I will wind up my business as quickly as possible and get there as rapidly as I can. Come up to my room and I will show you where I was sitting when the message came."

We went upstairs. On the table in the centre of the room the plans for the big office building were lying open, a chair had been thrown back and had fallen several feet away. Mr. Beyfus put it back in its place, took the plans again in his hands just as he had done perhaps only an hour before; Mrs. Beyfus, with the tears streaming down her face, stood behind him.

Some distance away in the window was the dressing-table with a very long mirror across it from side to side.

" I was sitting in this position with the plans before me, about to telephone to the contractors to go ahead, when for some reason I looked up and saw those words forming themselves across the glass. I read them but once—but once was quite sufficient. I threw the plans down and rushed from the room."

" If you only saw them once," Mrs. Beyfus sobbed, " it may easily have been a trick of your brain. You have been worrying over those plans for months; it is all imagination."

The moment of silence that followed seemed like an eternity. It was broken at last by the man at the table. " I know it is true," he said, and added slowly : "*The words were in my father's handwriting.*"

Taking up the 'phone, he called up the contractors. "Beyfus speaking. Yes, yes, Reuben Beyfus! Do nothing more on the plans for the office building. I have altered my mind—I will not go on with them. Send me in your account for what you have done," and he hung up the receiver with a crushed expression on his face.

I uttered what comforting platitudes I could and left them.

About ten months later, Mr. and Mrs. Beyfus, with their son Harry, called on me in London. Mrs. Beyfus looked tired and worn out, a very different woman from when I first met her in Boston only a year previously. Mr. Beyfus, on the contrary, looked remarkably well.

"Yes, I am feeling all right," he said in reply to my question. "I have striven to banish that uncanny incident from my mind. Once I got all my business affairs settled up and got on the boat, I gave my nerves a good rest. Now I am looking forward to my trip across Europe on my way to Jerusalem."

"You are really going there?" I asked.

He smiled.

"Of course I am, my friend. Once I have made up my mind nothing will alter it. If I am wrong, well, so much the better. In any case it would have taken something in the nature of the warning I got to have made a man like me give up business. If nothing happens, we can settle down in Europe and enjoy life better than we could do in Boston."

.   .   .   .   .

I never met Mr. Beyfus again. Some months later the son, Harry Beyfus, visited me, and told me the rest of the story.

After they reached Palestine they visited various points of interest in connection with the history of their race, but in the end Mr. Beyfus got impatient to reach Jerusalem before the 10th of April—the day on which he told them the twelve months fixed by the warning would be completed. In the last stage of the journey one delay happened after the other, so that it was *on the morning of the 10th that they finally arrived in the Holy City.*

"My father," Harry went on, "was as happy as a man could be."

All day long they went from place to place, wondering at the past history of their race, thinking over the inscrutable laws of destiny of which their people had been a more marked example than any other.

When evening came they had a light repast served in their own apartments, after which Harry and his mother went down to the office of the hotel to send off picture postcards to home.

They had left Mr. Beyfus sitting in the armchair reading a paper. They were all extremely happy—*the dreaded day was passing fast, and nothing had happened.*

When they came upstairs again they found Mr. Beyfus in the same position in which they had left him, but the newspaper had fallen on the floor and he appeared to be asleep. They did not want to disturb him, so they went to the window and watched the crowds passing up and down the street.

It was only as the clock struck midnight that Harry thought it was time to waken his father. Going over to him, he said: "Father, it is time to wake up. You have a lot to see to-morrow."

A curious stillness seemed to have spread over the room, a stillness that seemed cold and chill even on that spring evening in Jerusalem.

There was no answer. Reuben Beyfus had had his wish granted. He had seen Jerusalem and had passed away, even as predicted by the ghostly message upon the mirror.

CHAPTER VI

WARNINGS OF DEATH

CARDINAL DE ROHAN'S DEATH DATE SHOWN TO HIM IN ADVANCE.
A DEATH WARNING IN MY OWN FAMILY. A GHOSTLY VISITOR WHO
BLOWS OUT A LIGHT.

UNCANNY warnings of death have always exercised a weird fascination over men and women. In the following pages I give instances of warnings that have come under my observation.

My reader may wonder how such an event as the one I have related in the previous chapter could possibly occur. For my own part I am disposed to adopt the theory of the celebrated Cagliostro, the prince of Occultists, who himself related a somewhat similar experience.

When Cagliostro was in Paris, he was visited by the famous Cardinal de Rohan, who at that time was meditating securing the favour of Queen Marie Antoinette by presenting her with the world's most wonderful diamond necklace. Cagliostro warned the Prince-Cardinal against the project, predicting that disaster would come out of it, and saying : " Take heed, Cardinal, for thy day of doom creeps on thee like a shadow falling over a sunlit day."

The Cardinal, in the full plenitude of life, laughed at the prevision of death. That night, while supping with Bohemer, the court jeweller to Louis the Sixteenth, and with whom he was discussing the purchase of the necklace, he suddenly grew pale as ashes, his eyes glaring into vacancy, fixing themselves upon the opposite wall.

" My lord Prince, thou art ill! " cried the jeweller in alarm.

The Cardinal set down his gold cup from which he had been about to respond to a pledge of happiness and prosperity offered him by the fawning Bohemer.

" There—there! Look, the pale hand writes——" And as if unable to bear the sight, he hid his face in the ample sleeve of his red robe.

The jeweller stared in the direction indicated. But he saw nothing save the voluptuous paintings of court beauties that adorned the walls.

" What ails thee, lord Prince ? " he asked solicitously.

The Cardinal looked up, averting his eyes from the wall, and moistening his lips with the wine.

" I saw a pale hand come through the wall and it wrote : ' *Louis de Rohan, Prince and Cardinal, to die April 6th, 1802.*' "

History records this as the death-day of

the Cardinal. To Cagliostro, to whom the story of the hand was repeated, the explanation was a simple one and confirmed his intense faith in his Occult lore. When Cardinal de Rohan visited him he explained, he divined by a study of his natal day and other signs, that April 6th, 1802, would be the fatal moment. And although he did not mention the date, by his wonderful power of thought-projection, he impressed it upon the subconscious mind of the Cardinal. Later, when the prelate supped and he sat at ease, the sinister message appeared before him, taking the form of a phantom handwriting that was already impressed upon him by the subtle art of Cagliostro.

Omens of impending death in a family, or given to some particular person as relating to their own departure, have always possessed a deep interest to myself. I have made investigations personally into several cases of authentic omens. Right down from the earliest history of the human family, the impending presentiment or actual warning of departure from this life has been a subject of solemn importance.

In my own family, as far back as I can trace, we have always had a strange warning of the approach of death.

Exactly twelve months to the day before some member of the family dies, no matter how far apart we may be scattered, the warning comes clear and distinct to every living member *except to the one who is to be called away.*

This unmistakable warning is always the same—twelve knocks on the head of the bed in which any one of us may be sleeping, *repeated for three nights in succession.*

It has been our custom on such occasions to communicate with each member of the family, and the question invariably takes the form of " Have you heard anything ? " Those who have heard, reply " Yes." *One* will reply, " *I* have heard nothing." *Exactly twelve months to the moment the first knocks were heard, the one who heard nothing passes away.*

The most recent experience I had of this was in the case of my own mother. I was about to leave London for the Western States of America, with the prospect of going on to Australia and being away for at least three years, *when the warning came.*

I at once wrote to some cousins—the last blood relations left—and they all replied : " Yes, we have had the knocks three nights running." *My mother had heard nothing.*

I cancelled my journey and with an anxious heart called on a doctor and put my forebodings before him.

He did not scoff, as doctors generally do in such cases, but came to see my mother and, after some preamble about the advantages to be derived from having a medical examination from time to time, he persuaded her to tell him whatever symptoms she had.

In a few days he reported to me: " I see no reason for you to throw up your business engagements and your journey to America. Although your mother is sixty-eight, she is as sound as anyone can be, and the probability is that she will live for the next fifteen to twenty years. The supposed warning you told me about cannot be anything but a delusion. Take my advice and don't think about it any more."

Thank God, I *did* think about it, and I had the satisfaction of knowing that by taking the warning I did not leave her, and was able to make that last year of her life perhaps one of the happiest she had.

Exactly twelve months to the day, after a most unexpected illness, she passed away.

In connection with her last illness, I am now going to relate an incident that happened shortly before her death.

I would hesitate to make such things public if I did not believe that they are so evidential of the continuance of life after death that they may do something towards stemming the tide of materialism and bringing comfort to those who have lost some loved one.

There are thousands who have no real or tangible proof of the future life in their own experience, *but they long to have it,* and so it may be that, in making public some of those things that I have myself experienced, I may be giving to others the proofs they need to keep the lamp of hope alight in their own hearts.

There are some things we all hold sacred, and above all the last days and hours of those we have loved. I would not, therefore, for any reward in this world, unveil the last moments I am now going to speak of, except with the hope that by doing so I may be able to " throw a life line ". to some poor soul who in the stormy sea of doubt has lost faith and belief in the life hereafter.

A few weeks before she passed away, my mother had asked me to send for her niece, to whom she had always been very devoted. This lady came over from Ireland and promised my mother she would remain with us for some time.

The two doctors believed the end would come at any moment, but my mother lived on week after week—*the twelve months' warning had not run its course.*

One morning a letter came from my cousin's husband. He had been suddenly taken seriously ill, and he wanted her to return at once. Very troubled as to what she ought to do, we sat talking it over in the dining-room after dinner. The nurse had been to tell us that her patient was sleeping and not to come until she called us.

We were talking over things very calmly and very practically—just two people turning over what to do for the best.

We had finished dinner, the servants had

cleared the table, but still we sat on talking. From the centre of the ceiling hung a heavy iron pendant containing an incandescent gas lamp that was lighted, or lowered " to the blue," by a heavy brass chain being pulled up or down.

I had just made the remark : " If we could only get some definite idea how many weeks or days mother will live, you could go over and see your husband and perhaps return in time."

The words were hardly out of my lips when one of the chains on the pendant in the centre of the ceiling was slowly but steadily pulled— the room was plunged in darkness for a second ; then the other side moved, the lamp lit up again, and this was repeated three times.

" Does that mean," I said aloud, " that mother will only last three days ? "

For answer the light went down again three times and then remained as if out.

I went to my room for my calendar. We saw that in three days *the twelve months' warning would have run its course.*

In exactly three days my mother breathed her last.

In another family that I have known for many years, the warning appears in the form of a sinister-looking figure of a white-haired woman who appears in the dead of night by the bedside of each member of the family in rotation. The one who does not have the visitation *is the one who is to die.* By holding out the number of fingers of her right hand the figure indicates the exact number of months in which the death will occur.

An intensely gruesome feature of this warning is that the ghostly white-haired visitor appears at the bedside with a lighted candle in her left hand. With the index finger of her right, she touches the sleeper's face and *forces the person to wake up and look at her.*

She then proceeds slowly and methodically to show by the number of fingers she holds up, the exact number of months that will pass before the Dread Angel will take the loved one away.

Four fingers may be held up, three, two, or one, but of the many instances in which I have been able to investigate this phenomenon *the exact time has always been given.*

The end of this warning is unmistakable in its dread significance, and always takes the same form. The ghastly spectre, without any expression of sympathy or compassion in her face, looks for a moment at the lighted candle in her left hand and *slowly and deliberately blows it out.*

PART II
GHOSTS THAT ARE BIDDEN

" *I am absolutely convinced of the fact that those who have once lived on earth can and do communicate with us.*"

SIR WILLIAM BARRETT, F.R.S.

CHAPTER I

MY FATHER SPEAKS TO ME THREE YEARS AFTER HIS DEATH, AND
TELLS ME WHERE TO FIND DEEDS OF GREAT IMPORTANCE.

AT one time in my life, like many
others, I did not believe that the
Dead could return. In the following
pages I relate an experience of such far-
reaching importance to my own life that it
compelled my belief that communications
with the so-called dead are not only possible,
but, as in my own case, have practical value
beyond any question of doubt.

In March, 1896, in the West of America,
I received a cable saying my father was dying,
and urging me to return to England at once
if I hoped to see him alive.

Owing to my continual travels I had not
seen him for upwards of fifteen years.

Within a few hours of the receipt of the
cable, I was on a train making my way as
rapidly as possible to catch the next boat
sailing from New York. At each stopping-
place I cabled my father that I was coming.

It was a long journey, over 6,000 miles, but,
finally, I reached his bedside at 2 o'clock one

morning to find him still living. The doctor said that my cables had kept him alive. After the first greetings were over, speaking very faintly, my father said : " My son, I have used all my will-power to keep living in order to be able to tell you certain things about your family which I should have told you many years ago. God grant that I may have the strength to make up for it now."

Propped up by pillows and scarcely able to speak, he told me as rapidly as he could many facts that I had not known.

" There are papers valuable to you," he gasped, " in the hands of a firm of Solicitors in London. You must get these deeds as quickly as possible. The name and address of where they are has failed me for the moment. Lift my head a little higher ; open the window, let me get more air ; perhaps my memory will come back. My dear boy, forgive me. Like many others, I have left things until it is too late. No, I can't recollect, I cannot remember."

The effort was too great. Paralysis had already seized the upper part of his body— the poor tongue tried to speak, but no sound came. For four hours the eyes still lived and were fixed on mine, but at dawn the end came and he passed away with his secret.

* * * *

My life was a full one. I had no time to worry about old papers. I was always a fatalist—" if they are lost, they *are* lost "—

that's all I thought about them. Besides, youth cares little for musty deeds and claims of the dead. In a few weeks I had returned to America and did not think anything more about them.

Three years later, back in England again, I found myself one Sunday afternoon waiting at a Railway Station on the outskirts of London for some friends to join me from the South. Word had just come in that the train I expected was delayed and that there would be a good three hours to wait.

It was a dreary suburban station, on a wet Sunday evening. There was no book-stall open, not a paper to be had ; nothing to be done but to sit in the waiting-room and kick my heels for three long hours.

Vainly I looked round for some scrap of reading matter to while away the time. I would have been grateful for anything.

Suddenly I espied in the corner something that looked like a paper, and I pounced on it at once.

I laughed as I opened it—imagine anyone reading such trash I thought—but I was soon looking it over and reading it myself. It chanced to be a journal called *Light*, a paper devoted to the interests of Spiritualism in England, and there among the notices of meetings, on that very Sunday afternoon, in the prosy little suburb where I was stranded, was an announcement that at 4 o'clock at his house, close to the station, a séance for materialisation would be held by Mr. Cecil Husk, the blind medium.

" What fun! " I thought. " I may as well go round and see what these people do as wait on the station for three hours." By the help of a policeman I found the house, rang the bell, and with as meek an expression on my face as I could command, waited to see if I would be admitted.

The door was opened by a genial-looking elderly woman. " I see by this paper," I said, showing her the one I held in my hand, " that Mr. Husk is giving a séance at 4 o'clock. I am a few minutes late, but I would like to attend it."

She smiled a welcome, and said :

" We have just commenced, but there is room for another, so please come in."

Leaving my hat and coat in the hall, I followed her into a room rather dimly lighted, and sat down in a circle of people, briefly apologising for being a few minutes late.

The séance started with a hymn—the well-known "Lead Kindly Light" which was extremely well sung by the six or seven persons present. Before the last verse had ended, a pale floating light made its appearance and beat time to the rhythm of the tune.

" Very easy to fake that light," I thought. " Of course it is phosphorescent paint, or something of that sort," and I became still more hostile in my scepticism.

The medium sat immediately opposite to me, and there was sufficient light in the room from a shaded night lamp to distinctly see his face. He seemed an oldish man, rather feeble, but with a very kind expression.

Soon I began to be aware of some presence forming itself directly opposite my face—it came first as a kind of thin veil through which I could still see the figure of the medium. Then it got stronger and more opaque, and at the same time something soft and cold passed as a hand across my face and patted me very gently on the head.

"More fake," I mentally said, and wondered how they did it.

Just then the medium said: "The person opposite me is drawing a great deal of power; some spirit seems anxious to manifest to him. Let us sing again and give him all the vibrations we can."

Again a hymn was sung. Before the first verse had finished, I saw a face forming itself within a few feet of my own. Another verse and it became still clearer. Then slowly and very distinctly the well-known features of my dead father began to appear.

I was a sceptic—*still a sceptic*. There was no welcome from me, no apparent recognition —I was only trying to solve how it could be done; but how they could have got that wonderful likeness of my father surprised me.

I stared straight into the eyes of the

apparition, but in mine I knew there was no welcome. My whole feeling was: " I am not going to be made a fool of," and so I said aloud: " I wonder whose this face is opposite to me—it must come for somebody else."

While I spoke it had vanished. A half sob or sigh was distinctly heard in the room. I leaned back in my chair quite contented with myself. But my contentment did not last long. Close to my cheek something whispered: " *My boy, I have come only for you.*"

The person sitting next to me, whom I afterwards knew as Sir Wm. Vavasseur, said: " Somebody spoke to you, sir. Did you hear what they said ? "

" No," I replied. " I did not hear." The dim light in the room prevented others seeing the flush of anger on my face at the lie that escaped my lips. I felt inclined to leave the room and asked: " How long is this séance supposed to last ? " when, as if determined to make *one last effort*, the apparition formed again, but more distinctly than before. Every line in the face became visible, the head down to the shoulders took on a solidity that was amazing. My father had had heavy, black eyebrows and they were now knitted across his brow with an expression of determination and will-power that he only used when roused to make a great effort.

He had also a peculiar white mark on his nose, caused by an accident. This appeared clear and distinct as the face came now closer still to mine. A part of a hand developed and the first finger tapped on this mark as much as to say : " Now can you help but recognise that?"

In spite of all my scepticism I had to give in. There was such an expression of longing in those eyes that it was cruel not to answer them. Leaning forward I said : " Yes, father, I do recognise you ; but still I cannot believe it is really you. How can such a thing be possible ? "

I could see the lips trying hard to speak. The effort was so like that last moment when the nerves became paralysed before he died, that with the thinking of it the tears came into my eyes.

Then the voice came—so faintly at first that I could hardly catch the words.

The persons near me in the circle could see the face as clearly as I did. They could also hear the words, but instead of showing curiosity—I give them due credit—their only wish seemed to be to help. To give more vibrations they softly sung in harmony some hymn tunes, one after another ; they united in leaving me alone with the spirit face that they saw was trying so hard to give me some message.

My father's face came still closer to mine. I could now hear every word he was saying. The same voice as in life, *the same accent, the same intonation.* First a few words of ordinary greeting—just what a father would say to his son after not seeing him for some time.

".I am glad you are looking better, my boy, than when I last saw you at my bedside; but after that long journey to get to me it was natural that you were tired out. Tell your mother that I spoke to you to-night and tell her that your sister seems very happy over here, I only see her from time to time as her interests and mine are not the same. But I must not waste time, I must get back to where I left off when I was dying. You remember, my boy, at that critical moment when I tried to recall the address where your papers are, that my throat became paralysed, and I could not speak.

"How I have longed for this opportunity ever since—it seems ages ago to me. How I have blamed myself for leaving things till too late; but thank God, now I may be able to tell you. Listen carefully—I may not be able to repeat what I want to say. Go to a narrow street near a church in the Strand—I cannot remember the name of the street, it is fifty years since I was there. Search on the left-hand side for a brass plate bearing the name of Davis and Son, Solicitors.

"They have those papers; take them away with you. Forgive me, my boy, for being so careless about such matters. I cannot say more now. I have taken up a lot of time and there are others anxious to give messages to their friends. Please thank the people here for helping me by their sympathy."

" How did you know I was coming here, father ? " I asked.

" I did not know, only since I died I have been longing to tell you what I was not able to say on my deathbed. Yes, longing, my boy—and also praying. Prayers are answered over here just as they often are on the earth plane. Somehow to-night I was drawn here, *how, I do not know. I seemed to have followed a ray of light that had your face at the end of it.* That is all I know."

" Father," I said, " I will come here every night if you will only speak to me again."

" No," he answered. " I have done what I wanted to do. I will perhaps come to you again, but when, I do not know. I have given you proof of the after life, *such a proof as I never got.* Be thankful. By asking for too much one often loses all. Good-bye, my dear boy, good-bye."

The next morning, when shops and offices were beginning to open, I was already in the Strand. I easily found the street indicated, it was Holywell Street, very close to St. Clement Danes Church.

Going down on the left-hand side as I thought I had been told, I looked at every brass plate I could find. I went back again, but it was no use—there was no Davis and Son, Solicitors, to be found. I was almost in despair. I had even begun to doubt—I must have been hypnotised, I concluded, by that blind medium, and made to see what was, after all, in my own brain. Of course, I could have called up the picture of my father—after all, it was only three years ago he died. And then his voice, his accent, his intonation—I must have been hypnotised, I again asserted, and I cursed myself for being an imaginative fool. I could see it all so clearly now in the cold light of the morning, in the increasing roar of the traffic going up and down the Strand.

I was just about to hail a cab and drive home, when the thought flashed through my mind—could he have meant the left-hand side going West, and not the left-hand side going towards the city. Almost reluctantly I crossed to the other side of the street. I looked at every door. Half-way down I stopped—could I believe my eyes! On a small brass plate with the name almost rubbed out by years of the charwoman's polishing, were the words " Davis and Son, Solicitors, 4th Floor."

I groped up the creaky wooden stairs, pushed open a door, then an inside one, and found myself before a dried-up-looking old man in a dingy, badly-lighted room, seated at a desk with piles of papers tied in red tape before him.

" What do you want ? " was the gruff greeting I received.

" Sir," I said, when I could get my breath,

" my name is so-and-so. I understand you have papers in your possession belonging to my family—that is why I have called."

" What name did you say ? "

I repeated it.

" Never heard of the name before," he growled. " You must have come to the wrong address," and without another word he turned back to his deeds.

I was baffled. I did not know what to do, but just as I turned to go, a tottering old clerk came from an inside room.

" Becker," the man at the desk shouted, " did you ever hear of such a name ? The gentleman declares we have deeds belonging to that name. I never heard of it."

Becker twisted his small eyes towards me, searched his brain for a moment, and said very solemnly : " If you had asked me that question last week, sir, I would have said ' No '; but, a few days ago, in clearing up the cellar of old papers you took over with the practice of Davis and Son, I have a recollection I did come across that name."

" We will have a search made ; come back in a few days," the man at the desk looked up and said.

" Please, could I have them looked up now," I pleaded.

" Impossible. Come back in a week."

I went outside on the landing and waited, I hardly knew why.

To my astonishment, Becker, the old

clerk, came out and half-whispered: "Do you want them badly, sir? If so, I'll try and get them."

"It will be worth a five-pound note to you if you find them," I said.

"Five pounds," he said slowly, then he repeated it, and mumbling "five pounds" all the way down the stairs, he beckoned me to follow.

Without wasting words, I will briefly state that at the end of half an hour's search we found the papers which had been lost sight of for years. I returned to my home with them as quickly as possible, and after such an experience I do not think people can wonder that I, for one, *believe in communication from the other world*.

Rightly or wrongly, I have never been a member of any Spiritualistic Society, or any sect dealing with Psychic matters. I have kept my independence and have no "axe to grind" or religious movement to push forward; but from that date, 1899, I have had unusual experiences in such matters and now for the first time I think it is my duty to give these records to the public.

CHAPTER II

A BARGAIN MADE WITH A GHOST

In this Chapter I give details of my own experience in a Haunted House in the middle of London, and how I obtained peace by making a bargain with the Ghost who claimed the house for its own.

I AM prevented from giving the name and address of the house in which the following story was enacted by an old English law which provides severe penalties for any person who may in any way damage " the reputation of property."

After I gave up the house in question I was warned that if I put in print the address in recounting the strange occurrences that took place, I would be sued for heavy damages.

As I have every reason for believing this threat would be carried into effect, I am compelled to not even mention the street in which this house is situated, but as a proof that this story is a true one, I have lodged with the editor of the London Publishing Company full particulars and evidence to prove that what I relate is exact in every particular.

91

After one of my long world-journeys, I decided to settle down in London and remain in the heart of the great metropolis for at least some time.

A suitable house was, however, difficult to find. I wanted trees and a garden. I also wished to be in the centre of active life, and such a combination was not an easy one to find.

One afternoon, at the end of an unusually warm summer, by a mere chance I came across exactly the type of place I required.

It was an old-fashioned house, standing back from the main thoroughfare, with quite a large garden and several high trees that sheltered and concealed it from the passing traffic.

No agent had given me the address. There were no bills up, " To be Let " or " To be Sold," yet I intuitively felt that I should make some attempt to get possession of this house which so attracted me.

As I have all my life tried to follow my intuitions, I at once determined to make an effort to get particulars about the property.

There would be no harm to make inquiries, I thought.

I pushed open the high, old-fashioned, heavy oak door that cut the place off from the street, and as it closed behind me, I found myself in an instant in quite another world.

Outside the roar of omnibuses and traffic,

inside the high walls peace, quiet, and a strange feeling of old-world isolation.

In the centre of a badly kept garden a quaint fountain splashed and dripped as if Time for it had ceased to exist. By its side grew some bedraggled wallflowers and wandering nasturtiums, and further back was an old wooden seat in the last stages of decay.

The house itself, with its low diamond-shaped windows, looked gloomy and foreboding, yet there was something about it that appealed to me so strongly, that, without hesitation, I went up to the porch and pulled the chain of a heavy iron bell.

Instead of a servant answering as I expected, an elderly gentleman opened the door. For a moment I was completely nonplussed, and hardly knew what to say. Then I rattled off some excuse about having heard that the house might be let.

The old gentleman, although rather deaf, was very courteous, but firmly replied that I had made a mistake. I was turning to leave when his wife came out of the hall.

" My dear," he turned to her, " just imagine this gentleman calling to ask if this house is to let."

I again attempted to apologise for my intrusion, but was cut short by the lady saying :

" How you could have heard such a thing, sir, I do not know, but although I have not mentioned it to my husband, I have been thinking of putting the house in some agent's hands. Will you come in?"

With a happy smile I gladly assented. We entered an oblong, quaint looking, lounge hall. I glanced at the wooden beams across the ceiling, the dark oak panelling nearly black with age, the wide open hearth and Tudor-shaped fireplace—then, rather hesitatingly, the lady pulled aside some curtains and disclosed at the farther end, a small chancel or chapel with a stained glass window at the farther end.

"How delightful, how reposeful!" I instinctively exclaimed.

"I am glad you think so," she said. "We don't like the idea of the chapel so we keep it curtained off, but come and see the rest of the rooms."

Before we had gone very far I had mentally decided that I would take the house if the terms were at all suitable.

"Why do you want to get rid of the place?" I asked.

There was a curiously questioning look in her eyes as she replied:

"The trouble is, no servant will stop, no matter what I pay them. I will not try to deceive you, the servants' rooms are in the back, the old part, they hear noises, queer knocks and sometimes they think they see things; lately the knocks have begun in the other rooms. My husband is so deaf he does not hear them, but it has got on my nerves, and I will be glad to go if I can get anyone to take over the lease."

Then she added : " We have not been here long. My husband came in for this house on the death of his uncle twelve months ago. He was a very eccentric man and lived alone for many years with his old butler in the front part. The back rooms he would never allow anyone to use."

To make a long story short, within less than half an hour we had come to terms, but with the stipulation that the house would be handed over to me empty at the end of a fortnight.

The day came for me to take possession. I was as happy as a child with a new toy. There was something about the place that appealed to me in an extraordinary way. I walked through the dusty rooms and told them out loud how I would have them done up, how the old oak would be taken care of and polished, and the diamond-paned windows cleaned as they had not been done for years. I am not the only one who has felt that way over a house, I am quite sure.

There was one room, however, I would not touch. It was in the old part of the building off the stairs below the level of the hall. What there was about this room I could not explain; no suggestion I made seemed to fit in with it, and the decorator I had employed was equally at a loss what should be done, so in the end I turned the key in the door and left it as it was.

At last the day came when I could begin to send in some furniture, and as quickly as I could I fitted up two rooms, one for my secretary, a man twenty years older than myself, and the other for my own use. By living in the house I argued I would be able to get rid of the decorators more quickly than coming to see them every day.

At this stage I had no occasion to trouble about servants, as we could get our meals outside and simply sleep in the place.

Did I say sleep ?—from the very first evening such a thing was impossible. The first night my secretary and I got home about ten o'clock. We went through the basement, saw all doors and windows properly fastened, we groped our way through the decorators' ladders in the hall and little chapel downstairs and, turning off the electric lights, we got up into our rooms.

The place was as quiet and still as if we were in the middle of the country. The hum of the traffic in the distance had a soothing effect on one's nerves, like the sound of waves rising and falling on a sanded shore.

I had an electric light over my bed, so I read for a while, then switched it off and turned over to sleep.

I felt very happy about the house, the decorators were doing their work quickly, and I could see in my mind how everything would look when they had finished.

Suddenly I jumped with a start. Away down in the bottom of the house *there was a noise*—it sounded like the opening and shutting of a door in the basement.

Rapidly my mind went over all the doors and windows we had fastened. It must have been the wind I thought, then I remembered how still the night was, and how as I passed up the garden I had noticed that there was not a leaf stirring on the trees.

Again I heard a noise—this time I sat up in bed and listened intently!

There could be no mistaking now what I heard; *it was a heavy footstep on the basement stairs leading up to the hall.*

Sitting bolt upright in the dark I listened. The steps entered the hall. I imagined I could see someone walking in and out of the decorators' ladders, then they sounded nearer, and *the footsteps came to the uncarpeted staircase leading to our rooms.*

I could hear my heart beat—and yet I felt I dared not switch on my electric light. Curiously enough, I reasoned that if I did, the gleam under my door might lead the mysterious " steps " direct to my room.

The staircase creaked. I remembered as I came up to bed noticing a loose board in one of the treads—it was on the landing turning towards my door. It seemed ages before the footsteps came nearer—whoever it was did not seem in any particular hurry.

The loose board was reached—it made exactly the same noise as it had done when I walked on it on my way up to bed—a few more steps *and the shuffling feet were at my door*.

How strangely one's mind works in a moment of tension. I knew I had fastened the heavy brass bolt, I knew it would resist a good pressure when the pressure would come, *as I felt sure it must*. I wondered if the man outside were broad-shouldered, what he looked like, if he would wear a mask and a hundred other things of a like nature passed rapidly through my brain—but never for one moment did the idea come to me that the person outside my door *was not human*.

I hardly dared to breathe. I slipped out of bed, gripped a heavy iron poker from the grate, and with the other hand on the electric switch, waited for the bursting open of the door.

Instead, something came, which, to my excited senses, seemed a thousand times worse.

Suddenly, as if from knuckles made of bone, a sharp rat-a-tat tat, tat tat, rang on the centre panel of the door. I could feel my hair stand on end—the fright of the human had passed—in its place came the *terror of the supernatural—the dread of the unknown*.

Again came the heart-chilling knock, rat-a-tat tat, tat tat. I switched on the light, I do not know what possessed me. I rushed to the door, I pulled the bolt—threw it wide open and stood facing what . . . *blank darkness of an empty landing and nothing more.*

I gave a sigh of relief—for answer came something that made my very blood freeze—*by my side in the bright light of the electric lamp on the open door about level with my head*—the rat-a-tat tat was repeated *clearer and sharper than before.*

Jumping back, I slammed the door with a bang that echoed down the empty stairs. I shot in the brass bolt; shivering with fright I sat down on my bed and waited—waited for what I did not know.

Morning came at last, and with it courage. As the first streaks of Dawn stole gently through the windows I pulled up the blinds and welcomed the sight of a creaking horse-drawn omnibus passing in the distance.* A hansom cab, with its tingling bells, came along, looking for a fare. London woke up rapidly; workmen going to their jobs, then clerks, then typists, city men and others, the stream of Life thickened and flowed on rapidly; but how good it all looked, how real, how human, after the horror I had passed through but a few hours before.

Yes! With the light came courage. I put

* This happened in the days before motor-buses had made their appearance.

on my clothes, opened the door of my room
and stepped out on the landing.

How perfectly natural everything seemed;
the morning sun was streaming in through the
windows, the uncarpeted stairs seemed to
welcome me, the loose board made me jump
for a moment as it recalled the footfall of
the night before—but it was only for a moment, the next I was laughing at myself for
having such things as nerves.

I did exactly as so many others would
have done under similar circumstances; I
told myself, and in very forcible language,
that I was nothing more or less than a darned
fool to have allowed myself to imagine that
I had heard footsteps coming up those stairs,
and as for believing that I heard that rat-a-tat
tat on my door, I told myself that any man
who could work himself into such a state as
to think he heard any such thing, was only
fit for the nearest Lunatic Asylum, and
that, even, would be too good for such an
idiot.

At that moment my secretary opened his
door.

" Well, Perkins, did you have a good
night ? " I asked.

" *Did you* ? " he grunted.

" Certainly," I laughed. " I let my nerves
run riot; I heard footsteps coming up the
stairs; I heard a rat-a-tat tat on my door;
I sat up shivering on my bed all night and
generally made as big an idiot of myself as

a man ever made. Nerves are wonderful things, aren't they?"

"It's easy to laugh now in the bright sunshine," Perkins growled, "but I'm damned if I stop in this house another night for you or anyone else, sir; there's no money in the world would make up for it, that's all I've got to say."

"Well, if you heard so much, why didn't you come to my assistance?" I said, rather sharply, as that moment when I stood at my open door gazing into the blank landing passed like a flash across my memory.

As I looked at Perkins' wizened face, I realised it was no good trying to persuade myself that what I had heard was mere imagination.

Here was a level-headed man of the world, twenty years my senior, who had heard all I had heard, and *who was honest enough to admit that he was frightened out of his wits.*

"Well, my friend," I said, "what are we going to do about it?"

"There's nothing to do except to give the house up, give the keys back to the people that had it, ask them to return the money you've spent on it; if they don't agree quietly, bring them into Court, and I'll guarantee there are no twelve sane men that won't give a verdict in your favour."

"All very fine, Perkins, but let me point out, the lady told me she could not keep a servant in the place, that they heard knocks and noises; she admitted the place was haunted, I took it at my own risk, where does your twelve men's verdict come in now?"

"Well, sir, what are *you going to do*?" he asked.

"I'm going to keep the house, whatever happens," was my reply, "and, furthermore, I'm going to keep you, Perkins. Yes, I am, my friend. You've too much good old North of England blood not to fight it out to a finish, even with a ghost."

*　　*　　*　　*

That night we returned to the house about ten o'clock. We lit a fire in my room, put two easy chairs before it, we fortified ourselves with sandwiches, and good strong coffee, and determined to see things out till Dawn.

The first few hours passed quietly enough, about one o'clock we were dozing off to sleep in our chairs—suddenly we started up —there was no mistaking what we heard—a shuffling footstep on the landing—it came nearer—it stopped at the door—a pause—it seemed an eternity—then clear and sharp a determined rat-a-tat tat on the middle of the door.

We jumped from our chairs, we stood staring at one another like two helpless children, without a word.

A sharp click came from the empty

landing—*the electric light had been switched on.*

" Great God! that can't be a ghost." Perkins said.

We each took a heavy iron poker from the grate. I pulled back the bolt and threw the door open as I did the night before.

This time the landing was flooded with light.

Gripping tightly our iron pokers we stepped out on the stairs. Silence everywhere—a deadly silence at that.

I peered over the banisters, "Perkins," I whispered, "the lights are on in the hall, we can't leave them like that, *we must go down and turn them off.*"

Side by side, step by step, we went down together; we went very slowly, our feet seemed like lead—what we expected to find I do not know.

" It can't be a ghost with such light about," Perkins kept repeating as if to keep up his courage.

We stood on the last step of the stairs—before us the hall was flooded with light—*every lamp was on.* On our left the dining-room door wide open—the room in black darkness; we looked at the shining brass electric switches in a row just inside the door—something called our attention to them—then click, click, click, *one after the other they were switched on before our eyes,* and the empty room became a blaze of light.

We felt rooted to the spot, but it was only for a moment—out there somewhere in the middle of the empty room, yes out there under that silent gleam of light, we heard a hollow croaking kind of laugh—a sneering laugh that chilled our blood. It came closer to us—we almost felt it—we did not wait for more—with one bound we had reached the landing and were behind the closed door of my room.

*   *   *   *

When the decorators came to their work, they found all the lights on even down in the basement; we let them think what they liked about our carelessness, for neither Perkins nor myself were in a talkative mood. We were glad to go to our beds and sleep—and we did sleep as two men never slept before, and chiefly, I think, on account of *the human exquisite racket painters' ladders made on such an occasion.*

Night came again, after a good dinner we both felt quite courageous.

" Well, Perkins, are we going to see it through ? " I asked.

" I'm game for anything you wish," he nodded. " Only I don't mind telling you that I've smuggled a dog into my room for to-night, and if there's anything human about that ghost, then God help him, that's all I can say."

" What's the breed of this wonderful animal ? " I laughed.

" A thoroughbred mongrel, governor, a cross between an Irish wolfhound and a Scotch terrier, and born and reared in Yorkshire."

" Excellent," I said. " But suppose our ghost has no legs, what then ? "

" I've never heard of a ghost appearing *in the light* like last night," Perkins went on. " I can't yet believe that it wasn't a human hand that pulled down those electric switches, but you and I were in such a blue funk we couldn't think straight."

" What about the footsteps coming up the stairs ? "

" That's just it—they were too real to be those of a ghost," he went on. " Aren't we taught from our cradles that spirits have no substance, intangible things that float on air. No, sir ! My belief is that our ghost is a human scoundrel that wants to get you out of the house, and all I wish is that I may be able to get a London 'Bobby' on his track."

" So that's where your Irish-Scotch mongrel comes in ? " I laughed. " He's got to hold the ghost by the leg while you get the policeman, that's the plan, is it ? "

Perkins nodded assent. He was quite happy with his scheme. I must admit I was not quite so confident as we closed the garden gate behind us and looked up at the dark windows of the empty house.

I had had experiences with dogs before, when ghost hunting on previous occasions, and I had often noticed that animals showed more terror than even humans when they came in contact with anything that was uncanny or supernatural.

Still, as I put the latch-key in the door, there was something very comforting in hearing a vigorous barking from the room Perkins slept in, which continued while we switched on and off the lights and came up the stairs.

The poor animal went mad with delight to see us. He had been lonely, shut up all those hours—perhaps the sound of our voices was as much music to his ears as his vigorous barking seemed to ours.

We first allowed him to devour the supper we had brought him, and then boiling over with courage, and that " brave Horatius feeling " that men get when they have a dog for a companion, we three proceeded to the basement to see that the doors and windows were closed and fastened.

Our dog friend seemed afraid of nothing. He sniffed and barked in every room. He got smells of cats, rats and painters, but he was so intelligent, I am quite sure, he did not mix them up.

There was one place, however, where his Irish-Scotch blood got a set-back that puzzled even him. We had been out in the yard seeing that the heavy iron bar was across the door leading into the back alley. We had returned into the passage and had shot the bolt home in the inside door, remarking as we did so, that bolts in the days that house was built, were certainly not made for ornament. We had examined the windows in every part and had reached the threshold of that small room on the half-landing that up to then the painters had left untouched.

Calling the dog to follow, Perkins struck a match. It was the only room in the house that had no electric light. Perkins called again. The dog answered with a whine; he was crouching down on the door-step, *every hair standing up like a bristle, and trembling in every limb.*

The match went out. In the grey moon-light the dog's eyes looked twice their size, as if they were starting out of his head. His joy of life was gone, he was nothing more than a shivering mass of nerveless flesh, that could only answer his master with a whine.

We went up to my room, the dog following close to our heels. He was still trembling. I threw a cushion for him close to the fire; as I patted his head, he licked my hand, as if he wanted to thank me for that human touch.

"What do you think of your dog, Perkins?" I could not help but say.

He did not answer. He poured me out a cup of coffee. I took the hint and did not pursue the subject.

We had been sitting quietly for some time,

the distant hum of the streets had died down, a neighbouring clock had struck one; the house seemed very still, even the dog at our feet had gone to sleep—I was about to suggest that we should follow his example. Perkins started up.

" What was that ? " he whispered.

I shook my head. I had heard nothing. I looked at the dog; he was sitting bolt upright, but with ears lying down at the back of his head; he was evidently remembering the fright he had had a few hours ago.

I was beginning to think I was the bravest of the three—but away downstairs came the ominous sound of feet.

I could hear them entering the dining-room—then the hall—I could hear them stop at the foot of the stairs, then come on with a tread far more heavy and distinct than on the former occasion.

Perkins and I instinctively grabbed the two iron pokers, the dog stood between us, with his head back sniffing the air.

Suddenly a bang on the door—this time, thank God, accompanied by a human voice —and a pretty rough one at that.

" What the Hell's going on in this house ? "

The dog was already at the door barking like fury. He was evidently afraid of nothing that could use such straightforward English. Perkins got him by the collar. A heavy push made the door tremble—the brass bolt flew off, the door shot open—and there stood before us the finest sample of a London " Bobby " that my eyes ever saw.

He certainly looked particularly good to me at such a moment. I could not have greeted a god with greater fervour, but Mr. " Bobby " was not having any sentiment at such an hour. He was decidedly out of temper.

" What the Hell's going on in this house, I'd like to know ? " he repeated.

We hardly knew what to say. He went on :

" Five minutes ago your back door was closed and barred, I had just tried it on my first round when I heard the bolt being drawn and the door opened before my very eyes. I entered the yard, found the passage door open, every light in the place on, and you two gentlemen and a dog alone here in an empty house—what's the game, that's what I want to know ? "

It was no use trying to look dignified under such circumstances. I knew it would be still less use to attempt to explain " psychic phenonema " with an angry policeman at such an hour of the night, so I meekly said that my friend and I had not carelessly left the back doors open as he had imagined. We had very carefully bolted them before coming upstairs and there was no explanation that we could offer for their being found open.

" Well, I've got to search the house from top to bottom," he said. " There must be someone concealed on the premises that you don't know about, so come along with me and bring the dog."

We searched the house from the attics to the cellars, the Policeman's "bull's-eye" shooting its beams into every corner. The dog followed us all over the house except in the small room off the stairs where he had his previous fright. Into that room he absolutely refused to go. Each time we tried to induce him to enter he lay down crouching on the door-step trembling in every limb.

Mr. " Bobby " jotted remarks in his note-book as he would have to make a report about finding the doors open, he said. We finally saw him out into the back alley—put the big bolt back into its place and returned to my room. Nothing more happened that night. When daylight came Perkins retired with the dog, and I went to bed.

Whether it was the effect of Mr. " Bobby's " visit or the presence of the dog, I cannot say, but for a few weeks after that we had no disturbance of any kind.

One afternoon Henry Hamilton, the Dramatist, dropped in to see me.

" I quite envy you having this quaint old house in the heart of London," he said. " But tell me, have you had any queer experiences in it since you have taken it over ? "

" What kind of experiences do you mean?" I queried.

" Well," he went on, " when some friends
of mine lived here a few years ago, they
heard noises and knocks all over the place,
and on that account they gave the house up.
I will write down and place in an envelope
a message spelled out to me by knocks in this
very room. You will lock it up in your desk
and not open it until at some time a message
is again rapped out—then compare the two
and let me know if they are alike."

I promised I would do this, but as some
weeks went by without any knocks or dis-
turbances taking place, I had forgotten
about this envelope, until one night my
attention was drawn to it in a remarkable
manner.

I had asked a few friends to dinner, a kind
of " house warming " party, about a month
after I had got settled. After dinner we sat
round the fire in the Lounge, having coffee
and cigarettes, when for no apparent reason
a series of decided knocks commenced on
a crystal bowl containing flowers that I
always kept before an image of Buddha at
the far end of the little chapel.

Someone suggested that we should sit
round a table and ask the ghost to spell out
his name.

I took a writing-pad and a pencil, and
turning to where the knocks had been heard,
I said aloud :

" I will call out the letters of the alphabet,
please make a knock at the letter you want.

At the end I will read out the words. If they are correct rap three times, if not correct, rap once."

The message that came out clearly and distinctly was :

" My name is Karl Clint. I lived here about a hundred and twenty years ago. If you go down to the empty room off the stairs you will hear more."

Taking our chairs we moved to the empty room—the same room which, it will be remembered, the dog that Perkins brought would always refuse to cross the threshold.

As there was no electric lamp in this room, we placed a candle on the mantelpiece and sat round a small table we had brought down with us.

We had hardly taken our places before the knocks again commenced, this time much stronger than before, and on the centre of the wall immediately above where the candle stood.

The message that came was :

" I am Karl Clint. I own this house. In this room I murdered Liddel, I buried him underneath."

" Who was Liddel ? " I asked.

" He was Arthur Liddel."

" Do you want us to do anything about it ? "

" No! You can do nothing."

" Do you want any prayers said ? " someone asked.

" No! " very emphatically.

" Can we help you in any way ? "

" No! I want to be left alone in my own house. Why can't people keep away ? "

This was followed by a loud bang on the door, and at the same moment the candle was extinguished. In the darkness we groped our way out and were only too glad to get upstairs.

I opened the sealed envelope in my desk. It was almost *word for word with what I had taken down.*

*   *   *   *

The next day I looked up the archives and records of the parish. I found that between 1740 and 1800 the old part of the house had been a kind of farm owned by an Austrian or German named Karl Clint. This man had been mixed up with the disappearance of Arthur Liddel, who was last seen in the company of the man Clint. Years later all trace of Karl Clint had been lost. The farm had become covered with streets and the property had changed hands many times. The records gave me no further information.

Things had gone on quietly in the house for some weeks until the time came when I made plans to make some use of the empty room in question. The first thing I did was to put in electric light. That night I was awakened several times by knocks on my bedroom door. Two of the servants had also heard them and had immediately given notice. I telephoned my friends and asked them to come over that evening at nine o'clock. I had determined to solve the mystery one way or the other as to continue to live under such conditions appeared to me impossible.

I had had some experience of the results that could be at times obtained by the materialisation séances given by a blind medium named Cecil Husk. I determined to have this man with us to see if we could get something more tangible than messages given by knocks. I had some time previously attended séances where this man was the medium, at which forms developed and spirit voices of persons I recognised had spoken to me.

Perhaps, I thought, it will give the ghost who haunts this house an opportunity of showing more definitely what he wants me to do.

I should here explain that from the peculiar life I had led for so many years, and from the hundreds of confessions that men and women had poured into my ears, I had lost all sense of prejudice or the desire to judge or condemn any person for no matter what crime they might have committed.

Sinners and Saints had become alike to me. In both there was evil and in both good. The Sinner might have become the Saint if circumstances had been equal, and the Saint might as easily have been the Sinner if he had been exposed to the same temptation.

So it was that I would as gladly have helped the spirit of this self-confessed murderer, Karl Clint, as I would some long dead Bishop struggling to break the chains of Purgatory.

Nine o'clock came, my friends were punctual to the minute, shortly after I saw the blind medium being led up the garden path. I went to meet him and helped him into the dining-room where chairs had been placed round the central table.

I put the medium in the middle of the group. I switched off the main lights leaving a small lamp with a red shade burning at the far end of the room.

I had scarcely reached my seat opposite the medium before manifestations commenced in the shape of very decided knocks on the ceiling, the chandelier and a mirror hanging on the wall. Distinct footsteps were heard *apparently coming from the unused room*; they stopped at the door—a grey kind of shadowy cloud formed inside—it grew thicker—it came directly over to where I sat. Then out of it a head and shoulders formed and in another second I was looking into the face of Karl Clint.

I knew it was Karl Clint. He had no need to repeat his name. That weary, haunted, broken look, told me in a flash his loneliness, his heart-weariness ; and, murderer though he may have been, my soul went out to him in sympathy and pity.

Everyone could see the face I was looking

at. It was decidedly a German or Austrian type of head; as the features developed more clearly one could almost distinguish the texture of the skin and see the reddish colour of the hair and close-cropped beard.

In appearance the face was that of a man between forty-five and fifty years of age—an intelligent looking man, but of the peasant or farmer class.

Perhaps on account of the sympathetic look in my eyes the face in a few moments became still clearer. We could see that the lips were making a tremendous effort to speak. Several times they opened, but no sound came. At last, and how it was accomplished I can offer no explanation, *a voice did come*, at first only a kind of whisper—we strained every nerve to listen—a few guttural words came, then more, until every person in the room could hear the following conversation :

" Why are these people in my house ? "

" They are my friends," I answered. " Won't you tell me something about yourself ? "

" I am Karl Clint," the lips said. " I lived here as far as I can make out one hundred and twenty years ago, but time makes no difference to me now. It is people who appear to change. Why have you come here?"

" Because I liked your house. Perhaps I can help you by living here," I answered quickly.

" No one can help me," the voice said, in a curiously sad way. " I only want to be left in peace."

" But you are not at peace. If you were, you would not come and frighten people as you do."

" I can't get away, *since the night I died I am here all the time.*"

" You told us you murdered Liddel—why did you commit such a crime ? "

" Liddel would not leave the woman I lived with, alone. I loved Charlotte more than man ever loved a woman. He was always coming here tempting her with his money. One night he went too far. I killed him as I would a mad dog. People call such an act murder, but I would do the same over again if he and I were living. I dug a hole in the earth under the room downstairs. I filled it with quicklime. I put his body in it and what is left of it is there still as far as I can tell."

" What became of Charlotte ? " I asked.

" She died a few years later. She helped me to get rid of the body, but she never got over the worry and the dread of my being found out—I buried her in the graveyard not far from here."

" And what became of you ? "

" After she died I went back to Germany. I never knew a moment's happiness after Charlotte went—life for me was torture—in the end I committed suicide."

" And then ? "

"I can't tell you how it came about, but one day I seemed to wake up in the room downstairs and I've been here ever since."

"But would you not like to leave the place and get away?"

"Why should I? This was the only place I called home. I was happy here with the one woman I ever loved. It was *the only happiness I ever knew*, why should I leave—there is no place else for me to go."

"But Charlotte?" I blurted out.

"Charlotte is here with me. We live the old happy days over and over—till Liddel comes—*and then I kill him again.*"

"But surely there is something I can do to help you," I could not help saying.

"There is *one* thing you *can* do," the voice replied. "Leave the room downstairs untouched. Put two chairs and a table there, and allow no one to enter it after dark. If you will do this, you can have the rest of the place for yourself and I won't give you any trouble."

I pledged my word I would carry out my side of the bargain. That night two chairs and a table were placed in what I now called "his room." I locked the door and put the key in my safe, and from that out I had no more annoyances or noises of any kind.

*   *   *   *

Some years passed, the day came for me to give this house up and live in a different part of London.

A few evenings before I left I thought I ought to have another séance—out of sentiment, perhaps—to say good-bye to my ghost friend, who had so faithfully kept to his side of the bargain.

Without much waiting Karl Clint again appeared.

" Karl," I said, " I am moving to another house. I thought I would like to say good-bye and thank you for having kept to your side of the arrangement. For the last time I am going to ask is there anything I can do to help you before other people take over this house ? "

To my very great surprise the answer came clear and distinct :

" *I want to go with you*, you are the only one I ever met who has shown sympathy with me. Behind the panelling in my room you will find a painting I had made of Charlotte. I put it there when she died and it has been hidden there ever since. Take it with you, hang it somewhere in your home, and perhaps when the time comes for you to pass into the shadow-land, you will have at least two humble but loyal friends to greet you."

*　　*　　*　　*

I found Charlotte's picture behind the panelling—it is on the wall over my desk as I write this manuscript.

" Upwards of one thousand of the so-called dead have materialised and appeared at circles where I have sat during the past five years. I have looked into their faces, and received messages from their spirit voices."

JOHN LOBB (thirty years Editor of *The Christian Age*).

CHAPTER III

NURSE CAVELL SPEAKS TO ME TWO YEARS AFTER HER EXECUTION

SHE EMPLOYS ME TO CARRY OUT SOMETHING SHE WANTED DONE, AND PRODUCED CLEAR EVIDENCE OF SURVIVAL AFTER DEATH IN A REMARKABLE MANNER.

THE notes I wrote down at the time of this remarkable séance were witnessed and signed by those present, and have been handed to the Editor of this series as proof of the facts I am about to relate.

It was the afternoon of Monday, the 8th of October, 1917. Boom! Boom! of the guns protecting London. Crash! Crash! of splinters of shells falling on the roofs—we were in the middle of an air-raid in the worst days of the War.

We had had little rest for the four previous nights and were beginning to feel the strain on our nerves from the want of sleep. I turned to my wife and said : " We can do no good here : suppose we take the train to our country house and have a rest for at least a few days. There is a train at 6 o'clock—in an hour we shall be at all events out of this awful din."

Just then the telephone rang. A voice said : " Will you let me come up to your house ? I am alone here in my rooms and terribly upset with the raids of the last few nights. Do let me come."

I recognised the voice, and answered : " We are tired out ourselves and going to our place in the country for a few days. Pack a few things in a valise. We will be happy to take you with us if you will come up at once."

" Thank you, so much, I will come now."

The voice was that of a woman, one of the very many remarkable mediums I have come across.

On our way to the station we called for two other friends who were also glad to get away, and a little over an hour later we were far from London ; and in the quiet of the country soon forgot the nerve-racking experiences of the previous nights.

The medium was as pleased as a child would be with the change. " I only wish I could do something for you to show you how grateful I am," she said.

We were sitting in the windows of a large lounge dining-room waiting for dinner to be served. Outside, the birds were still singing, the scent of the flowers floated in from the garden. Night had not yet come—it was summer time and the rays of the Autumn sun shone like the glint of rubies across the sky.

"I do wish I could do something to show you

how grateful I am for this peace," the medium said again.

She had hardly finished speaking when we noticed that the flowers in the central vase on the dining table had begun to move—the table was fully twenty feet from where we were sitting—the movement soon became very decided; several roses appeared to be lifted out of the bowl and fell on the polished oak table. For a few moments we sat and watched without speaking. Then to our amazement the roses slowly, but steadily, moved across the table till they reached the lace mats at each place where we were going to sit. (This happened, it must be remembered, in no dark room, but with sunlight shining through the windows.)

The medium broke the silence. " It is evidently a message to us from our Spirit friends," she said. " They must be glad that we have come out here to peace and quietness. I know now what I can do to show how grateful I am. Let me give you my services every evening while I am here. I will be only too happy to do this."

Then commenced a series of séances in our own house in some ways the most remarkable that I ever experienced.

In the following pages I can only give the leading features that may be of general interest, and will avoid all personal matters as much as possible. Furthermore, I will relate in simple language the plain facts as they occurred, without any attempt at word-painting or straining after effects. And, lastly, as the Editor of this series can bear testimony, the account of each séance is signed by the persons who were present. These witnesses are living and can substantiate any statement I may make.

After dinner we went upstairs to a room that I determined to keep apart as our regular meeting-place, and perhaps out of a sentimental idea, which I think many readers will understand, we brought up all the flowers from the dining-table and placed them in vases in this room. That was the only preparation we made except to give orders to the servants that we were not to be disturbed.

Before I enter into a description of the remarkable incidents I am about to relate, it is, I think, only fair to those readers who know nothing about such matters to give them some idea of how these séances were conducted.

In the first place they must disabuse their mind that there is any kind of Black Art, or Magic of any description, connected with them. They must also realise that persons like myself and my friends are serious, sober-minded people, with just as much keenness of brain and determination not to be subjected to trickery or delusions as would be any other members of the community.

Further, there is nothing anti-religious in such meetings. I have attended séances with Mohammedans, Brahmins, Protestants, Roman Catholics, Jews and members of other sects. There is nothing antagonistic to any form of religion, but I have always asked that the religious element at each séance should be preserved; that the Brahmin, the Catholic, the Jew, or the Christian, should at least unite in some expression of prayer to the God we all worship, that we might be permitted to penetrate, in no matter how slight a way, into the mystery of life that surrounds us, and so perhaps gain even a little insight into what is known as "the Life beyond."

A few words of some simple prayer, that is all. It does not matter if the words are spoken by a Catholic, a Brahmin or a Jew—it is *the Thought that is the principal thing.*

Then, as it is a well-known law in nature that the tones of the human voice set up vibrations in the atmosphere, so Music is generally used at these séances. It is also a well-known law that once vibrations are started no one can tell where they end, and so it has been found by experience that Music, and especially that of the human voice, is more or less necessary. For this reason singing is generally resorted to, and some hymn or song that those present know is generally used both at the commencement and at intervals during the séance.

Bearing in mind these few remarks we will now return to where I left off.

We had seated ourselves in the form of a circle, and sat quietly waiting to see if there would be manifestations of any kind.

In passing, I may here explain that the special form of mediumship of the medium who was with us is what is known as " the direct voice," namely a voice is heard speaking to some individual member of the circle or in many cases to all present at the same time; and this voice, or voices as it may be, can be heard high above the heads of the circle and heard by everyone at the same time, or it may be so close to the ear of some member as to be heard by that one person alone. In many cases I have heard as many as four or five voices speaking at the same moment, and on several occasions in distinct and different languages, such as French, German, Italian and English; and if persons who understand other languages are present, in even Greek, Russian, Arabic, Hindustani, etc.

In some cases "the voice" is so faint that an instrument like a trumpet is used, made of either aluminium or papier-maché, and at these séances for " the direct voice " there is generally one placed in the room. I have, however, attended many séances where " the voice " has been so loud that every word has been heard outside and for a long distance beyond the séance room.

The remarkable part about this form of communication with relatives or friends who

have passed to the great beyond, is that as a
general rule the voices are easily recognised;
the same accent, intonation, or tricks of manner being faithfully reproduced. Further,
the " spirit voice " if there is a doubt as to
its identity recalls events in the past with
startling accuracy.

The one puzzling point that is difficult of
explanation is: that though one may desire
ever so earnestly to speak to some one
special person, this intense desire appears
very frequently to act as a determent and
prevents the phenomena.

It is often when one ceases to be anxious,
and becomes indifferent to any special desire,
that at the most unexpected moment the
voice of the person one has wanted to hear
for so long suddenly breaks through, and the
spirit will describe accurately how many
séances one has attended without result. The
spirit will often add: " I saw you on each
occasion and I knew how you desired to hear
me, but yet I could not get through—*I
cannot explain it.*"

Another peculiar point is that those who
are often complete strangers to one, come
back time after time and use some person
present to send messages to their friends or
relatives still living. It may be some sympathetic link of magnetism that may cause this,
but it has never been clearly explained. I
have often asked why this was, but the same
answer was always given: " I cannot ex-

plain. Perhaps I am able to do this on account of the vibrations that those present are attuned to."

At the séance in question, I have said that we sat quietly waiting to see if there would be any form of manifestation. On this occasion we had not long to wait. A curious floating light almost at once made its appearance and came directly to where I was sitting. Speaking clearly and distinctly, and so loud that everyone in the room could hear, a voice began addressing me and said: "I am Edith Cavell, or you will know me better as Nurse Cavell who was, as of course you have read, executed in Brussels."

"Yes," I answered, "I read what the newspapers said about your trial and subsequent execution. Like thousands of others I sent my heart out in sympathy to you," and I continued to say a few more things that anybody would probably say if they were to suddenly talk to Nurse Cavell.

Then the wonder part of it, why she should come to me, flashed through my brain, and I impulsively added:

" Why do you come to me, Nurse, of all people in this world ? "

For answer there was a slight laugh, just as if she was enjoying a joke at my expense: " Why ? just because you are a friend of Doctor So-and-so and I want to get to him, and can only do so through you. Is not that a good reason ? "

"Yes, in one way," I said; "but if you can come to me why can't you influence him?"

Again a quiet laugh. Then very distinctly the words came: "You know as well as I do what a sceptic he is about such things. *I could not get through to him.* You will see him to-morrow. I want you to tell him that I spoke to you to-night, and give him and his wife my love."

"I fear he will not believe me," I said. "Besides, there is no reason why I should see him to-morrow."

"*Yes, you will see him to-morrow,*" she answered rapidly, "at 9 o'clock in the morning *he will be standing at the foot of your bed,* and even if he does not believe you I want you to try. Surely you will make the effort for me?"

"Yes, Nurse, after the terrible ordeal you went through in Brussels I will be happy to do anything you ask."

"I only did my duty to my country," she replied. "I am only sorry now I did not take Doctor So-and-so's advice, as I would have been of more use to our poor men, but I knew well the risk I ran, and the end was not a surprise to me. When I came over here I met many friends, and later on Von Bissing, who was largely responsible for my execution. After he died I met him over here in what I suppose the majority of people call 'the other world.' I went forward and held out my hands to him. At first he kept his head down and would not look at me, but now he understands and we are quite good friends. Now *do* tell Doctor So-and-so that I have spoken to you. and that I would like him so much to come to-morrow evening as I want to speak to him myself. As he does not believe in these things he may get very angry. If he does, tell him that Edith Cavell told you the reason he was given by his Mother one of his names was——" and she whispered the reason into my ear so that the others present could not hear what it was. " Good-bye, I hope you will get the Doctor round for I will come here to-morrow night again."

*   *   *   *

I will pass over the other things that took place at this very remarkable séance as they were more of a personal nature.

I went to bed that night perfectly convinced that on one point Edith Cavell was wrong, namely, that Doctor So-and-so would be standing at the foot of my bed at 9 o'clock the next morning.

I slept well, but at seven o'clock I woke with a start. I sat bolt upright and wondered what was the matter. I felt queer and quite dizzy. I quickly realised that something was wrong with my throat. I tried to swallow, but could not do so, and then to my horror I realised I could hardly speak.

I threw open the windows and paced up and down my room in the morning sun. From an electric heater I drew hot water and tried to gargle my throat as best I could. Nearly an hour went past but I got no better. I was, in fact, getting worse. It was then I thought of sending for Doctor So-and-so. I beckoned the gardener, as he was passing the window, and made him 'phone to the Doctor to come as soon as possible, and got back to bed.

The Doctor came. "There is nothing seriously the matter with your throat, my friend," he said. "Why you can't swallow may be due to some form of temporary paralysis. Of course, I can give you relief, and I will do so at once."

A camel-hair brush and a little morphine on the end of it, did its work, and in a few moments I lay back on the pillows able to swallow and again able to speak.

Up to then I had not thought of the previous night—to be perfectly frank I had been too frightened about myself to think of anything else.

Just then the clock on my dressing-table struck 9 o'clock—the Doctor was standing at the foot of my bed with his arms on the rails.

Suddenly it all came back to me. "Doctor," I gasped, "Edith Cavell was speaking here last night. Nurse Cavell, I mean. She wanted me to tell you——" I could not finish the sentence, the Doctor's eyes were glaring at me.

"What! What!" he said. "Have you gone mad?"

"No, Doctor, I am as sane as you are; but I swear what I am saying is the absolute truth. Nurse Cavell, speaking last night, asked me to tell you. She wants you to come here to-night—she wants to speak to you herself—she wants to——"

"Enough! my good man. Don't talk such nonsense," and he put his hand gently on my head as if to calm me. "Edith Cavell herself would not have believed such rubbish. It's an hallucination you must have had last night. But why you should pounce on Edith Cavell I can't imagine."

"She told me last night," I went on, "that it would be next to impossible to get you to believe my story, but she wants to prove to you that life and intelligence go on after the so-called death and *she will prove this to you if you will come to-night.* She told me if you would not believe that, I was to tell you the reason you were given one of your names was——" and I repeated exactly what she told me.

The Doctor's face underwent a change. "I will come to-night at 9 o'clock," he said, and without another word left the room.

*   *   *   *

Nine o'clock had struck. There was no sign of the Doctor coming to the house. I had closed the outside door and the four persons who were present the previous night went with me upstairs. The room had not been touched since the night before. I had locked it up and the key had not left my pocket.

We took our places again, and we were about to sing a verse of some hymn when, without any warning, a voice said at my side: " Wait a few moments longer. The Doctor *is coming*. I would like him to be here at the commencement. Thank you so much for doing what I asked you to do. *He is coming up the garden now.* Go down and let him in."

I went downstairs and found the Doctor standing at the door.

" I did not know whether to ring or not," he said. " I am sorry if I am late, but I could not make up my mind to come. Tell me, what am I supposed to do."

" Nothing, my dear sir, absolutely nothing. You have only got to sit quiet. If a voice speaks to you just answer in common politeness as you would if somebody spoke to you in ordinary life."

We went upstairs together. The doctor took a chair next the medium (to watch that she played no tricks, he told me later).

Almost immediately everybody present heard a voice speaking very clearly and distinctly to the Doctor.

(In these pages I cannot, of course, give more than the general outlines of conversations that took place as a great deal of what is said at such a moment is too intimate and personal to publish broadcast.)

Very gently, in a very sweet but firm way,

the voice said : " I am so glad to see you here. I am Edith Cavell. I was not really sure you would come. I told your friend to tell you I had spoken to him last night, but knowing your views on these matters, I could not feel certain that you would come. You remember the correspondence we had ? I often wish now that I had taken your advice, for if I had I would have lived longer to have carried on my work. They sent you on all my letters, I think ? "

" Yes," the Doctor answered, " except the last one you wrote—the one before your execution—that has not reached me."

" You will get it one of these days," the voice went on, " and on next Friday you will hear a lot about me."

" I am going to meet your advocate, Maître Lavel, in London on that day," the Doctor said, " and I expect he will tell me a good deal about what took place."

" Two of the persons who were largely responsible for my death," the voice continued, " I have met over here since. It seemed strange meeting them."

" How did you meet them ? " the Doctor asked.

" Oh," she answered, " I went forward with hands outstretched. At first they did not seem to want to meet me, and held their heads down so as not to see me ; but I took their hands in mine and after that it was all right. I am going on with my work here just the same; you must not think of me as dead. It is so wonderful to be able to speak to you like this. Give my love to —— and tell her you have been speaking with me, and thank you again for your good advice and all you tried to do for me. What I principally wanted to prove to you is, *that the soul side of life goes on after the death of the material body.*"

After a moment's silence a flower floated across the room and was laid on the Doctor's hand. It had been taken from a vase on a table near the window.

I had written an account of the principal incidents as they took place, and at the end, before we left the room, everyone present signed the document as a true recital of what had taken place. The first person to put his name to it was the Doctor.

It is only delicacy of feeling that forbids my publishing his name; but, as I said at the commencement, the Editor of this series can testify that he has seen these documents, and that they are signed and witnessed as I have stated.

"*When an animal or person dies, the organism reverts to its elementary form, but the Soul, of which life is the external or visible manifestation, continues to exist independently of the body.*"

GEORGE LINDSAY JOHNSON, M.A., B.C., M.D.

"*The whole party including myself heard the chanting of a choir of male voices, which appeared to come from an open space where some debris marked the place where the choir originally stood. The chant was melodious and solemn.*"

Description of his visit to the ruins of the Abbey at Jumièges, Normandy, on July 6th, 1913, by ERNESTINE ANNE.

CHAPTER IV

A REMARKABLE PHENOMENON

Nurse Cavell comes again. King Edward VII gives a message, during the Great War. Wonderful spirit music is heard and the famous Nordica sang as she did when alive.

THE séance the following evening on October 10th was so purely personal to those who were present that I do not think it would be of sufficient general interest to publish the conversations that occurred, and so will proceed to the one of October 11th. At this séance Nurse Cavell came again and in exactly the same clear voice she used on the evenings of the 8th and 9th, she went on to explain the reason why she had wanted to speak to Doctor So-and-so, and thanked me for the efforts I had made to get him to be present. She spoke about certain wounded soldiers at —— Hospital. She added that she was present when Queen Alexandra visited it a few days previously, and that she tried to speak to the Queen-Mother, but was not able to do so.

She explained a great deal of how very different it was in "the other world" from what people imagined it to be, and that it was those who were really good-hearted, and who tried to do good for Good's own sake without looking for reward, who appeared to be so much more happy over there than those individuals who simply belonged to some church and who thought—that was all that mattered.

She mentioned she had met certain friends of mine and one relative who had been killed in the trenches a few months previously. And she added, as they knew something of " the life beyond " before they died, they were able to be of great help to those spirits who were suddenly transported out of the body, and who had in their lives thought little of such subjects. She gave the names of my friends who had died with great clearness and accuracy, and a great many particulars that it would not be of general interest to publish. Before she ceased speaking she said very decidedly :

" I wonder if you can understand that I help the German soldiers that pass over just as willingly as I do our own men."

After this, a deep voice broke in and said :

" Oh, men of the world, how little you understand the things that are around you. Even insects have more instinct than you have. The angle-worm provides for its food more than you do, and the blind ant stores up provision for the winter. But you men fight and kill one another in the name of civilisation."

Then a very different voice to the previous one said, very slowly and emphatically: " Pray for my country. Pray for my people. England has many dark days before her. I weep for my people—for the people of England. I was called ' Edward, the Peacemaker.' "

" Do you mean Edward the VII ? " somebody asked.

" Yes, I am Edward the VII—pray for England and for the British Empire."

Then turning towards me, the voice said :

" I am indebted to you, sir, for having told me the exact date of my death even to the month and the day, when I first met you many years before it occurred. Your warning made a deep impression on my mind, and through it I made preparations which I might otherwise have left till perhaps too late."*

I will now give an account of a remarkable phenomenon which occurred at the end of this séance.

I have mentioned previously in these pages *that at times voices join in with the singing.* It is hard, I know, to expect people to believe such a statement that actual voices are heard. There are, however, plenty of other investigators of this phenomenon who can

* This refers to the first time when, as Prince of Wales, I met King Edward VII at Lady Arthur Paget's house in 1891.

confirm that they also have heard spirit voices mingling with the singing at séances, but I have never heard any experience to equal the following :

On this particular evening I had placed on a side table an Edison phonograph, together with some half-dozen of the old kind of cylinder records. These I intended to use as a change in our usual musical programme.

I had slipped on a particularly good record from " The Tales of Hoffmann " and for a moment or so we leant back in our chairs and listened to the exquisite melody of that well-known score.

Suddenly, high up above our heads, we heard a soprano voice, clear as a silver bell, take up the refrain, then another voice and another and another, until we could not count them. The phonograph stopped, but the singing went on till the act of the opera was finished. Never, never, never had I heard such singing. The beautiful tones of the soprano's voice seemed strangely familiar to me. I leaned forward in the direction of where the last notes had faded away. I hardly dared ask the question I wanted so much to put. There was only one person in the world who could sing the "Barcarole" like that—passed through my mind—my dear friend Nordica. Could it be possible ?

Perhaps she read the question in my mind. Perhaps she saw the look on my face—I do not know. I only know that in another moment she was speaking to me, calling me " Cheiro " in the same old way she was in the habit of doing. " Yes," she said, " it is as great a surprise to me as it is to you. How it has come about I do not understand. I suddenly found myself here, heard the notes of the opera I know so well; it seemed so natural for me to sing it and it has been such a pleasure. But, I do not understand, *I do not understand.*"

For more than five minutes we talked. She told me about the shipwreck she went through, the pneumonia that followed, and how quickly the end came.

Suddenly she said in her quick imperious way : " You have always been interested in queer things, but keep quiet for a few moments : there is something else going to happen that is beyond anything I can imagine. There are many singers here—some I recognise, some I do not ; but there is a man at the present moment at the phonograph who is explaining that he is about to cause a phenomenon to take place that is contrary to all known laws of physics and also of music. He says leave ' The Tales of Hoffmann ' on the cylinder, start the instrument and see what happens."

I pressed the lever, the cylinder commenced playing. Then occurred something that nothing I know of can explain. I will simply put down the facts *as they occurred,* but I will take any oath given me *that these things did occur,* and that *they are written down exactly as they took place.*

The cylinder played about half a minute, when the soprano's voice *on the record* suddenly changed into a contralto, then a tenor, then a bass—the cylinder revolving all the time as before. When the portion of the chorus came, all parts changed, and yet kept the most wonderful harmony, the tenor at times becoming the soprano, the soprano the bass or vice versa. This phenomenon was repeated *twice over on the same record,* and then ceased.

Nordica's voice came again : " I cannot explain it," she said. " I can form no idea how it was done. The man tells me it has never been done before and perhaps never will be again. Yet is it any more wonderful than that I can speak and sing here to-night ? "

" Will you sing once more ? " I asked. " Perhaps I may never hear your voice again."

" I will try," she answered. " What do you want me to sing ? "

For a moment all her great rôles flashed before me, but one simple song stood out above all others. I had heard her sing it a dozen times, but I always wanted to hear it again. . .

" ' You gave me but a rose,' " I answered.

A moment's silence, then Nordica's voice

and *only Nordica's voice*, sang that song *as only Nordica could sing it.*

. . . . .

The séance had come to a close. We went downstairs and found many people in the garden who had been attracted from the roadway by the singing. They begged me to persuade the singer, whom they naturally thought was stopping with us, to sing that song once more over again. It was a difficult situation, I could only say that the singer had left.

" I tell you with all the strength and conviction I can utter, that we do persist, that people over there still take an interest in what is going on here; and are able from time to time to communicate with us."

SIR OLIVER LODGE.

Chap. xiv, *The Great Problem*, by G. L. Johnson, M.A., M.D.

CHAPTER V

A ROYAL ACADEMY ARTIST AND THE SPIRIT OF A MURDERED DANCING GIRL

LETTERS CORROBORATING THE FACTS IN THE FOLLOWING NARRATIVE ARE AMONG THE DOCUMENTS HELD IN TRUST TO PROVE THE TRUTH OF THESE STORIES.

SEVERAL of my experiences of the Uncanny have been in association with Miss Fanny Cooke, a medium who underwent hundreds of tests at the hands of Sir William Crookes, the famous scientist.

Incidentally I may mention that at one of these séances (at which I was present) the spirit of Lady Crookes appeared and made several communications to me, particularly referring to a " Phillip " of whom I knew nothing. I therefore wrote to Sir William, detailing the communication, and hoping he could shed some light upon it. The following is his reply :

> " 7 Kensington Park Gardens,
> London, W.,
> Oct. 15, 1917.

My dear Sir,

Pray accept my sincere thanks for your letter of the 12th inst., and for the messages from my dear departed wife. It is very blissful for me to get such messages.

All the information given or referred to is quite accurate. The 'Phillip' referred to was a brother of mine who died many years ago.

Believe me to be,

Very truly yours,

WILLIAM CROOKES."

Some years before the Great War I was often in the company of Robert W. Macbeth, a Royal Academician of great talent, who has since died. He was a man of extraordinary culture and charm. He would often discuss with me my professional work, but always taking care to emphasise he did not believe in anything of the supernatural or of Occultism. " Bosh! " was his terse summing up.

One evening I was dining at his house with him and his wife. It appeared from the conversation she had been reading a book on haunted houses, ghosts, and apparitions. I could not resist the temptation to add a few experiences of my own, having spent a good many hours investigating various " uncanny happenings " in old mansions throughout the country. From this the talk turned naturally to spirit manifestations, warnings of impending death, and other similar subjects.

Finally I related several instances that had come personally under my knowledge of those we call dead coming back and showing themselves to the living.

Macbeth waxed furious against such an idea, declaring that only " women and fools " could believe such things were possible. He declared that at séances people were humbugged by conjurers, and that no manifestation could be produced outside of the medium's rooms where there were, he contended, trap doors, hidden wires, and so forth.

" If you could get one of your mediums," he said, turning to me, " who would produce anything right here in my studio, that would be something to go by. But it can't be done. I know it can't be done."

I thought of Miss Cooke, with her extraordinary power for causing " materialisation " *to appear even in the light.* I had such a long series of experiences with her mediumship that I felt justified in taking up the challenge. The presence of this medium in any part of a house was often sufficient to produce the most unbelievable phenomena, even in rooms where she was not present.

But I also knew that whatever the magnetism or vibration was that caused such manifestations, it was something that could not be called on to order, and I had experienced some blank séances with her when nothing whatever happened.

It was difficult to know how to act with such a pronounced sceptic as Macbeth, for I realised if I sent for this medium and nothing happened that my friend would become a greater sceptic than ever—if such a thing could be possible.

" Would it satisfy you ? " I said, after a moment's reflection, " if I gave you a medium's name and address whom you could send for yourself ? This would avoid any appearance of collusion on my part. If this medium comes and gives you no satisfaction whatever—in fact, if nothing happens—you give her no fee. But if, on the contrary, even *one* spirit appears and proves to your satisfaction that it is the spirit of somebody you knew in life, you will in such a case pay the medium double for coming so late at night. Is that a fair offer ? "

" In other words—no results, no pay," Macbeth laughed. " Yes, that is quite fair. Give me the name and address."

I wrote both down. Macbeth went into the street, called a cab and sent for the medium.

It was only a week previously that General Sir Alfred Turner and I had been present in Sir William Crookes's house when not one, but several spirits had materialised and walked about the room in full light ; and from this and other experiences I had had with this medium under most trying and severe conditions, I felt convinced that she would not shirk or try to evade whatever test my friend Macbeth demanded.

The cab returned in half an hour with the medium. She entered the studio. I thanked her for coming and told her that my friend wanted her to give us a séance, but that she would have to agree to whatever conditions he imposed.

Miss Cooke, a fragile little woman, looked alarmed for a moment, for I must admit Macbeth's face was not very friendly or encouraging.

" Miss Cooke," he said, " I don't want to be made a fool of. I believe you mediums play all kind of tricks on credulous people. To come straight to the point, the test I propose is this : First, you go with my wife to her bedroom, leave everything you have there, put on her dressing-gown, return here, where you must allow me to fasten you into a chair and seal the knots with my own seal. Lastly, I will place your feet in a tub, half filled with plaster of Paris. When it sets I shall be satisfied that you can't move about and play any tricks. If under such conditions anything occurs, I will be so satisfied that I will give you double your fee. But if nothing happens, you will get nothing. I am not a hard or cruel man, but I won't be made a fool of. Do you understand ? "

Miss Cooke did not answer for a moment. Then, very quietly, she said : " You must realise that I can never *guarantee* to get any results—sometimes no matter how I try, nothing whatever happens. Although your scepticism is against surrounding me with the right atmosphere, I will agree to your conditions, but on account of your outlook on such a subject, whether anything happens or not,

I refuse absolutely to take any money to-night."

In about thirty minutes all was ready. Miss Cooke was tied up in an oak chair, the knots sealed by Macbeth's own seal, her feet to above the ankles set in plaster of Paris. We took our places in the far end of the studio close to a table lamp on the piano. Macbeth locked the door, put the key in his pocket and sat down beside me.

For fully ten minutes we heard nothing but the medium breathing heavily, and she appeared to be in a deep trance.

Macbeth, with a smile of satisfaction on his face, lay back in his chair smoking a cigarette.

Suddenly we all saw something floating in the air. The light from the lamp did not penetrate the far end of the studio which opened into the dining-room—slowly the object floated in.

Clearly and distinctly there appeared the form of a young woman. The head, face and body as far as the waist became very clearly developed—there was no mistaking the apparition was that of a young girl.

Moving forward, she came to within a few feet of Macbeth and then stood quietly looking at him.

"Monsieur," she said in broken English, " do you remember me ? "

" No," he answered. " I do not."

" You will when I tell you my story. I

have good reason to remember you. It is many years ago," she went on. "You came to Algiers. Do you remember the dancing Arab girl, Monsieur ? "

Against his will, as it were, Macbeth answered in a low voice :

" Yes, I do remember. But what mystery of the Unexplainable is this ? "

In her quaint broken English she continued:

" You remember making a picture of me. But jealous eyes were watching. My lover was waiting for me at the door, and heard me say I would come to your hotel the next day."

There was a pause.

" Ah, Monsieur, did you wonder why I did not come ? Now you may know. I was stabbed to the heart—killed by my lover, because he said he loved me so much."

The apparition faded, the voice died away. Robert Macbeth wiped his forehead with his handkerchief and looked around him with a dazed expression.

" This beats me," he said at last. " I had clean forgotten that episode in Algiers, and it must be years ago. I saw an Arab dancing girl, and I thought what a wonderful picture she would make. I found she had been a model for other English artists and could speak a little of our language. I made a sketch of her during one of her dances and got her to promise she would come to my hotel the next day. When she didn't turn

up I assumed she had found some other job.
I did hear some rumour of a dancing girl
being killed in one of the bazaars, but such
incidents are common in the native quarter.
But now I know the truth. *I have that sketch
still in my possession.*"

CHAPTER VI

THE HAUNTED HOUSE IN KENSAL RISE

MR. W. T. STEAD AND I HAVE A REMARKABLE EXPERIENCE. A MURDERER RE-ACTS HOW HE TRIED TO COVER UP HIS CRIME.

THINKING over my experiences of the uncanny, I should like to detail one that is of considerable scientific value, especially to students of criminology. I have not mentioned the exact number of the house or road where the incident occurred, to avoid alarm or pain to people who may be living there now.

The late Mr. Stead was, as is well known, acutely interested in anything connected with the supernatural and positively revelled in investigating haunted houses and mysterious manifestations of any kind.

On one occasion he called me up on the telephone and said :

"Cheiro, are you interested in a most peculiar case of haunting in a house associated with a recent crime? If so, meet me this evening, as I am going to investigate."

I went and met him and he quickly gave me the general outline of the story :

A house in Kensal Rise had been empty

for some weeks, and had been taken by a retired sailor and his wife. They were both quiet, highly respectable people. The man had been away at sea for twenty years and had decided to settle down. But they had not been in their new house long before they began to be continually disturbed. At evening and sometimes during the day would be heard a loud bumping noise. The first time the wife heard it she was alone in the house. She ran to the foot of the stairs, expecting to see someone coming down. But the noise ceased abruptly.

One night husband and wife were at supper when, without warning, the noise began again. Both ran to the end of the stairs. While they stood there they heard not only a measured bumping as if a heavy box was coming down step by step, but also the sound of heavy breathing. Then again all became quiet and they retired to the kitchen, puzzled to account for the extraordinary occurrence.

Now, the husband was a stolid man, " not afeard of anything," as he said. But very shortly after he and his wife left the house. The reason they gave was evasive, but it was understood the place didn't " agree with them."

The house was empty for a time, the rent was lowered, and there came a married couple with two children. They had come from Canada, being returned emigrants who had grown tired of the Dominions.

They, too, had been disturbed and alarmed by the noises. The climax came when one evening the little girl, aged six, called loudly to her mother. She ran upstairs. The child said :

" Mummie, I saw the gentleman to-night. He came by my cot and patted my hand."

The mother dismissed this as a childish dream. But for several nights the same thing was repeated. Then one midnight the bumping commenced louder than ever. Going to the head of the stairs, the husband felt a chill apprehension that he was not alone. The noise had ceased, but he distinctly felt something brush by him and a moment later the door of the bedroom along the landing closed with a bang.

" Now, Cheiro," said Stead, " the pair have flown from the house in a panic. The landlord has given me permission to investigate. I have the key. Will you come round with me ? "

I agreed, and we took a cab to Kensal Rise. It was one of those airless nights that one often gets in London in the early autumn. When we reached the house, we went inside and examined the place by the aid of two strong flashlights.

It was a house with a deep basement, two large rooms on the ground floor level, and upstairs two bedrooms and a small box-room having a tank-room above. I should judge the age of the house to be about fifty years.

There were no mystery nooks or winding passages; a grimly respectable Victorian house, and nothing more.

The stairs came down from the bedrooms to the ground floor and, with a short break, went down again into the kitchen. I understood from Mr. Stead it was on the lower pair of stairs that the peculiar noise was generally heard.

We made a fire of some wood we found and settled ourselves in the kitchen with the door open. The time passed slowly. Soon it was past midnight and I was beginning to nod. But suddenly I was shaken into wakefulness by Stead saying sharply: " Hark! Do you hear *that* ? "

I listened and there smote upon my straining ears an ominous sound. *Bump! Bump! Bump!* Then a pause and a distinct sound of heavy breathing. Collecting our wits, we dashed out and flashed our lights up the stairs. There was nothing to see. But as the sounds ceased, I could have sworn I heard a faint chuckling, ghastly and unearthly.

We went all over the house again and made a thorough investigation. We had left the kitchen door wide open; on our return it was shut. But this we agreed might have a natural explanation, as it could have been caused by some draught.

We continued our vigil. Nothing happened until daylight was creeping into the house, and by then both of us had fallen into a sound slumber. Starting up, the sounds were just as convincing as before. But we could find nothing. I must confess we were completely baffled.

It was then Stead told me something that threw a new light upon the haunting—for such I had formed the opinion it was. It appears that the house had been occupied by a man who had emulated the crime of Devereux. The latter, who also resided in the neighbourhood, murdered his wife and twin children and placed them in a trunk, sending it to a cloak-room " to be called for." It appears the tenant of the house we investigated also placed his hapless wife in a trunk, and was conveying it on a barrow to a railway station when a wheel came off. A kindly policeman drew near to give assistance, when the murderer, in a panic, fled and blew out his brains with a revolver.

In the light of this knowledge, I could understand the uncanny sounds within the house. The crime had been committed in the bedroom at the top of the flight of stairs leading from the ground floor. After disposal in the large trunk, the murderer must have, with infinite labour, lowered it down the steep stairs. The story of the child, of the apparition of the " gentleman " that appeared, was most significant; for it was disclosed at the inquest that the murderer was a quiet man and was *very fond of children*.

That houses have been haunted by great

crimes is unquestionable. It would seem that the tortured soul that has shed blood must return again and yet again, repeating its crime, unable to escape from the hideous bondage of repetition until Mercy cries *Enough!* and pardon is found even for the murderer.

Such investigations of the uncanny are of fascinating interest. The remorseful thoughts of the shedder of blood undoubtedly are at times bodied forth in *phatasmagoria*, assuming strange shapes or expressed by sounds. Thomas Hood, in matchless language, foreshadowed this idea in *Eugene Aram :*

" But now the universal air,
 Seemed lit with ghastly flame ;
Ten thousand, thousand dreadful eyes
 Were looking down in blame,
As I took the dead man by the hand—
 And called him by his name—"

Impelled by some terrible remorse, the murderer appears to be compelled to revisit the scene of the crime, rehearsing it over again and again.

The old prayer for the malefactor, uttered by the pious before the scaffold, assumes a new interest in the light of the foregoing : " Deliver him, O God, from the power of his sin ; break off from his soul the spell of blood-guiltiness."

CHAPTER VII

WARNING AGAINST THE GREAT WAR GIVEN IN THE DEATH-CHAPEL OF THE ROYAL HAPSBURG FAMILY

IN THE FOLLOWING PAGES I RELATE HOW WARNINGS OF THE COMING OF THE GREAT EUROPEAN WAR WERE GIVEN BY THOSE WHO HAD ALREADY DEPARTED THIS LIFE.

WHEN the Great War came thundering down upon a world drowsing in the golden sunshine of August, 1914, it seemed to catch civilisation unprepared. But there is ample evidence that before the arrival of this catastrophe, there were warnings given by those in "the Beyond"—persons who in their day had played an important part in the conduct of human affairs— desperately trying to warn the living of the carnage and ruin that was coming. I will illustrate this by the following experience I had in Vienna that was clearly a warning of approaching events of overwhelming importance, although I confess it was not till afterwards—when the guns were thundering and the god of War was taking toll of nations— that the full significance of these warnings was grasped.

In the early part of 1913 I was in Vienna.

I was called there in connection with an invention I was perfecting at the time.

When last in London I had had a visit from my esteemed friend, Count von Holtzberg, an aristocrat of German-Austrian extraction, and a sincere lover of international peace. This man was a great student of occultism and the supernatural, and was well versed in the many remarkable traditions of the House of Hohenzollern and the House of Hapsburg, the fall of which he knew had been foreshadowed by Zunklehorn, the Berlin mystic, although this prediction he characterised as "absurd." And such things did seem absurd in those days of peace and plenty.

When the Count knew I was going to Vienna, he particularly requested I should pay a visit to the Princess Zisky, a lady of mysterious birth (as he explained) who occupied in those days a rather peculiar position in high Viennese society.

Claiming to be a direct descendant of the father of the late Emperor Nicholas of Russia, her imperial aspirations were frowned upon by the Russian Court, and for this reason she had taken up her residence in Vienna. When residing in Petrograd, she had been associated with Heliodor, the mystic monk—whom I also met on one of my visits to Petrograd—and from him she had learned the elements of Occultism. Count von Holtzberg impressed upon me the fact that the

Princess was a mystic of remarkable power, and a natural clairvoyant who had had dealings with many important personages at the Viennese Court.

When, therefore, I found myself installed in a suite of rooms in an hotel in the Rathaus-platz by the Ring-Strasse, having little to do save sight-seeing, I thought I would make the acquaintance of the Princess. Her apartment, I found, was in the Leopoldstadt district in an old and remarkable-looking mansion dating back several hundreds of years.

The Princess Zisky I discovered to be an extremely handsome woman, with an expressive, clearly cut face. She received me in *bizarre* surroundings. In an immense and low apartment, with daylight carefully shuttered out, the only illumination was procured from a small silver lamp. She herself reclined upon a number of crimson cushions scattered over a low divan. Being sheathed in a tight-fitting garment of dark green, covered with sequins that glittered brightly, she gave me the impression of a sinuous serpent-woman as she stretched out a long arm, entirely bare, while the extraordinary length of her hand attracted my attention.

It did not escape my observation that a wicker basket on a nearby tripod had the lid slightly raised. Occasionally a flat and sinister head protruded and was withdrawn.

" Ah, yes," she said, speaking English excellently, for, as she told me afterwards,

she had spent a considerable time in London.
"I see *Tanitha* wants to welcome you."
With this she uttered a peculiar, bird-like
note, repeating it several times. A large snake
emerged, swaying from side to side, and
finally glided from the basket and coiled
itself round her. It was a full-grown Indian
cobra.

"Tanitha is my familiar," she said simply.
"He is a reincarnation of Ra Set, the Hindu
god of Wisdom who lived at Benares. I had
him given to me by a *Fakir* I knew well while
in India."

While she was speaking, Tanitha inflated
his ghastly hood (a flap-like projection at the
back of the skull) and hissed gently, while he
swayed to and fro in a kind of rhythm.

Her conversation was deeply interesting.
From the Princess I heard much of the
extraordinary fashion in which Rasputin had
got hold of the Czar and Czarina and of the
weird séances that were held in the Winter
Palace, at which it was said that the spirit of
Peter the Great appeared and warned the
Czar of his forthcoming doom.

We began to discuss prevision and premo-
nitions. Suddenly the Princess said:

"If, Cheiro, you are so interested in these
matters, as evidently you are, and *if you are
not afraid*, will you accompany me to the
Cathedral of St. Stephen this evening for an
experiment in 'spirit-raising' that I am
going to undertake? I warn you it is likely

to be out of the ordinary—but, there, doubt-less you are well used to such things."

I confess the project fascinated me, al-though I was not sure whether the Princess was not exaggerating her powers. However, late at night we sallied forth in the direction of the Cathedral of St. Stephen.

My friend the Princess explained that we were bound for the catacombs, one of the most characteristic features of this monstrous medieval building, and that she intended to enter the mausoleum wherein is the tomb of Prince Eugene of Savoy and many departed members of the Hapsburg dynasty.

"But, surely, Princess," I said, "you can-not enter the tomb-chapel. It must be guarded well, and besides——"

She interrupted me with a merry laugh and produced a small and peculiar key from her handbag.

"My dear Cheiro," she said, "as you have also practised the Occult you will know that the profession brings many helpful friends. I had the good fortune to tell some things to Baron Steiner (who afterwards became Lord Chamberlain to the ill-fated Emperor Karl) and I have the *entrée* to the catacombs and other tombs. Besides," she added mysteri-ously, "there is a secret passage leading from the catacombs to the Hofberg Imperial Palace, that lies to the south-west of the Cathedral. Some of the members of the Court have a fondness for séances wherein I

am called upon to show my art in predictions."

Thus chatting, we eventually came to one
of the many secret doors that lead down into
the mysterious, winding catacombs. One of
these yielded to a second key she carried;
and guided by a flashlight, we made our way
along the stifling passages on each side of
which were niches containing encoffined
death. A more eerie place I could not have
imagined.

After traversing some distance we were
stopped by a huge door of intricate wrought
iron. This also yielded to a key she carried.
Passing through, we were soon in the Mausoleum fashioned in 1513 for the body of the
great Frederick the III, while opening out of
it was the tomb-chapel of the illustrious
Prince Eugene of Savoy.

A solemn brooding silence oppressed the
habitation of the departed. The vivacity of
the Princess fled. She remained for some
time buried in thought as she took from her
bag a small candle and fixed it on a stand,
which illuminated the chapel or rather made
the darkness more visible by its feeble rays.

" Do you know, Cheiro," she said, breaking
from her reverie, " that the murdered Empress, Elizabeth of Austria, who was killed by
the Italian anarchist at Geneva in 1897, cher-
ished the belief she was the reincarnated
spirit of Elizabeth, consort of Prince Eugene.

" Before she was finally interred in the

burial vaults of the Capuchin Church, by a secret wish expressed in her will, her body was brought here to lie in state. She often said her spirit would haunt this spot."

She relapsed into silence. I gazed round upon the strange scene—the huge monument, the gilded railings, the escutcheon of the departed, and the mouldered flags.

Suddenly the Princess broke the heavy silence.

" Cheiro, do you believe the dead can be summoned back ? "

Before I could answer her, she had stiffened into an attitude of strained expectancy. Her eyes were vacant, gazing into space. Slowly she raised her long arms, then clasped her hands as if in supplication.

" Speak, O dead! " she cried in a high voice. " Speak, and let the Future be unrolled for those who yet live! "

There came an imperious knocking, repeated four times, upon the heavy door that separated the Mausoleum from yet another Royal Mausoleum that opened out beyond where we were standing.

I strove hard to remain in possession of my critical faculties. Still, I confess there invaded me a sense of the uncanny—the unbelievable. The setting of the scene was awful in its solemnity. And yet—! in a few moments I was conscious of a thin vapoury cloud that had appeared in front of the door. It floated forward, taking shape vaguely as that of a woman. It advanced nearer, swaying in the chill wind I felt passing across the chapel.

The Princess fell upon her knees.

"It is the Empress," she whispered. "Elizabeth of Austria."

By this time the phantom form was some few feet in front of me. I saw it was that of a woman, handsome and regal looking, robed in white and carrying a small cross in her left hand.

While we waited silently for the *dénouement* of this strange appearance, a voice filled the chapel. It was high and clear and echoed through the place:

"Sorrow of sorrows, was ever sorrow like to my sorrow! O bleeding heart of Motherhood transfixed by Death's arrow!"

Instantly my mind reverted to the crowning sorrow of the life of Elizabeth of Austria, when the tragedy of Meyerling Chateau robbed her of her son Rudolph, Crown Prince of Austro-Hungary, and I recalled how that dead son had first lain in state in this very chapel.

The voice continued:

"Woe to the world! Woe to the Mothers! For they shall weep like Rachel and refuse to be comforted. The time cometh quickly when the earth shall be drenched in blood and the nations shall destroy each other. The House of Hapsburg shall fall and mighty shall be its ruin! ”

Gradually the apparition faded until nothing remained. I shivered, for the vault of the dead seemed strangely cold and uncanny. The Princess remained upon her knees, a dry sob escaping occasionally from her lips. Then raising her head, she said slowly :

“ She has spoken again. What does it mean—War! But against whom ? ”

In silence we made our way out of the chapel and traversed the gloomy catacombs.

All around me were the evidences of mortality, while on my soul weighed the presage of the warning uttered by the dead—That the heart of universal Motherhood would be pierced, and that War must soon come upon the civilised world.

When I was once again in the apartments of the Princess we both worked out the significant years of Fate, and 1914 clearly was indicated as the commencement of some great conflict.

I cannot close this part of my narrative without detailing a remarkable incident associated with the tragic death of the Princess.

Before I left her she conversed somewhat fatalistically upon her death, saying sorrowfully she felt it would come before long. Then, as if trying to cast off her gloomy convictions, she said :

"But when it does come, Cheiro, *I will give you a sign that you cannot possibly mistake.*"

It was in November, 1916. I was in my house reading an old book upon Magic written by a long-dead seer. The dull afternoon was closing down to a cheerless night; I had neglected to switch on the electric light, and laying aside the book, sat watching absently the play of the red firelight. My mind was clairvoyant and receptive.

Without warning, I seemed to see, detaching itself from the glowing logs on the hearth, a snake, its sheeny skin glistening in the light. Fascinated, I watched as it slowly appeared to emerge from the heart of the fire, and then commence to make its way towards where I was sitting. I could not take my eyes from the loathsome creature as nearer and nearer it drew itself towards me. Just in front of my chair it paused, erected itself, with its beady eyes sparkling, swaying from side to side.

Across my mind passed one word : " *Tanitha !* " It was The Sign!

It came still nearer, the movements of its flat head growing wilder. Then, out of the haze formed the face of the Princess Zisky, appealing, wild, and unearthly. I cried out in terror—the spell was broken. I came back into reality to find the fire sunk low and the daylight swallowed up by night. So impressive was the incident, that I then and there noted it down in my journal.

A short time afterwards I received a communication from Count von Holtzberg. He wrote : " I have just heard that the Princess Zisky committed suicide in Buda Pesth. She killed herself with a pistol. Before she died she destroyed her pet snake."

The year previous to the Great War I attended a séance in London with Count von Holtzberg. Many friends of his who had passed into " the Great Beyond " came and spoke to him, but among others was an old German professor whom the Count immediately recognised as one of his teachers in his boyhood days. Very distinctly, but with a voice trembling with emotion, the old professor, speaking in German, begged Count Holtzberg to sell all his property in England and leave the country at once.

" I shall do no such thing ! " the Count replied. " I love living in England ; what do you mean by talking to me like that ? "

" I beg of you to do what I tell you," the professor answered. " There is only a short while left in which you can do it. England, Germany and Austria will be at war before a year will come to an end."

" Nonsense," the Count replied. " Such a war is not possible. Believe me, my good man, you have carried over to ' the other side ' your old-fashioned prejudice against England ; Germans and Austrians of to-day are not mad enough to dream of such a war."

Broken with emotion, the voice replied :
" Those whom the gods would fain destroy—
they first drive mad! I am not wrong.
Germany and Austria *will* be mad enough to
do it. I will tell more, at first they will appear
to win—they will drive all before them. Then
the tide will turn—they will be beaten back,
crushed back, crushed and humiliated. It
will be a long war, and the peace that follows
it will be worse than war."

Count von Holtzberg laughed at the idea.
He stayed on in England until it was too late
to get away ; he was in the first round-up of
Germans to be interned.

These were but two warnings from " the
Beyond " that came through against the
awful catastrophe that was drawing near. A
third concerned myself more personally.

On Thursday, August 14th, 1913, I attended a séance in my house. My mind was
very full of some big projects I had on hand.
Suddenly a spirit, who had spoken to me on
many occasions, broke in and said emphatically :

" You will not be able to carry out your
plans. England and all Europe are on the
eve of a long and terrible war. It will not come
till some time in 1914—but be prepared."

I did not believe, although I made a note
of the incident. I went on with my plans
until everything came to a standstill on the
outbreak of the War a year later.

CHAPTER VIII

GREAT GEM OF ILL-OMEN THAT FORESHADOWED THE DOWNFALL OF THE KAISER

IN THIS REVELATION OF A CURSE OF EVIL THAT WAS ATTACHED TO A FAMOUS GEM IN THE CROWN OF PRUSSIA, I REVEAL HOW THE KAISER'S DOOM, AND THAT OF HIS DYNASTY, WAS PROPHESIED MANY YEARS BEFORE THE WAR BY A GERMAN MYSTIC; A MYSTERIOUS SÉANCE IN BERLIN WHEN THE APPARITION OF FREDERICK THE GREAT UTTERED A SOLEMN WARNING.

DID the Kaiser know, long before his flight from Berlin, that his crown would fall from his head and his dynastic claims crumble into the dust of humiliation?

My reply to that question is an emphatic " *Yes!* " I can produce evidence that he was solemnly warned and specifically of the impending doom that hovered over him even when he was in the plenitude of his power. Moreover, on two occasions he deliberately provoked the Fate predicted, disregarding advice tendered to him and pretending to laugh at revelations of the supernatural that were indeed the writing on the wall.

In unravelling this enthralling story that, for various reasons, has never before been made public, I would emphasise the importance to be attached to the occult influence of precious stones. This is not the place to go exhaustively into the question of how strangely and strongly various precious stones affect the fortunes of individuals. But anyone who has surveyed ancient history will have been struck by the value attached to gifts of stones of price to potentates and rulers. Moreover, there is hardly a historic gem but has attached to it a chequered story of sudden death and intrigue.

England's own Koh - i - Noor, meaning Mountain of Light, can boast a long series of terrific crimes attached to its history before the spell was broken (as it was predicted it should be) by its passing from the East to the West.*

On January 27th, 1859, Fredrick William Victor Albert was born in the Schloss Palace, Berlin. Seeing that his mother was the Princess Royal of England, it was natural that Queen Victoria, after receipt of the news of the birth, should telegraph: " Is he a fine boy ? " The answer was in the affirmative; but it is now known that a deformity of the infant, a withered arm, was not discovered till afterwards.

The tragic death of his father after a three months' reign brought the Prince to the throne of Germany as William the Second.

---

* The Koh-i-Noor diamond was last in the possession of the King of Delhi, and after the suppression of the Mutiny was brought to England and incorporated in the Royal Regalia.

On June 15th, 1887, he was crowned King of Prussia and proclaimed Emperor of Germany.

For this ceremony the famous Iron Crown of Prussia was used—the weighty diadem that had encircled the brow of Frederick the Great. But the crown was not the same in spartan simplicity as when the Maker of Prussia placed it on his head. It had been beautified after the death of Frederick by the addition of a number of gems. *And in the centre, blazing with baleful beauty, was the glorious stone of evil fame: " The Eye of Bhudha."*

I must now pass on to a strange acquaintance I made during my professional career—a mysterious being concerning whom the wildest stories circulated in Germany and, indeed, throughout the Continent. I refer to Herr Zunklehorn, better known as " The Immortal."

I was tired at the close of the day's routine of seeing clients one late afternoon, when my secretary came in and said :

" There is a curious old fellow who wants an interview. He gives no name; looks shabby ; and is, I fancy, a foreigner. Shall I say you are too busy to see anyone ? "

Yes, I was tired and a little jaded. For the immense concentration necessary for my work had sapped my energy ; all that afternoon there had been a succession of men and women who demanded to know what Fate had in store for them.

" No," I said wearily. " I cannot see any-one." And then I paused. For drifting in behind my secretary, like some withered leaf blown in by the wind, was an old man. He came forward, and pulling off a broad-brimmed hat, tossed it on one of my chairs.

" Yes, Cheiro," he said, in a soft whispering voice. " You will—you must see me. As a disciple of Althus you will listen."

Althus! The name arrested my attention. For it was that of the great Greek seer who had devoted his whole life to the study of the influence of gems upon human beings. But could this shabby old man be the custodian of any secrets? Still, I had lived long enough to learn that the word of wisdom often came from the most unlikely mouth. Strange, too, my weariness seemed to have vanished. I was eager to know more of my visitor. My secretary discreetly left the room.

I could now see, as my visitor sank into a chair, that he was frail with extreme age. His bald, high skull, piercing blue eyes, curved thin nose, and well-shaped mouth, impressed me. Where had I seen such a face before? I remembered. I have in my possession a picture of that famous English astrologer and occultist—Dr. John Dee.

" Cheiro," he said, regarding me intently, " I have heard of you and perhaps you have heard of myself. Both of us have walked the same path, seeking the keys that shall open the doors upon the supreme mysteries of life and death. My name is Zunklehorn."

I recognised the name immediately as a man famous throughout Germany and the Continent for his predictions and also for his amazing researches into the history of famous gems. Strange rumours were afloat concerning his attainments and age.

The year was 1908. The previous August the Kaiser had met King Edward at Homburg, and in November the German monarch had visited England. It was a time when, on the surface, Anglo-German relations were being cemented by the efforts of William the Second, together with English Statesmen.

Zunklehorn talked of various matters and then said in his peculiarly soft voice:

" Cheiro, my time, as we reckon the years, is nearly spun from the spool of Fate. I shall soon be seen no longer. Before I depart I desire to put you in possession of certain facts that are of the highest importance, not only in the art we both cherish, but also for the countries we represent."

I nodded. I confess I was deeply interested.

" You know, I suppose," he went on, " how it was that I lost favour at Court ? " Seeing that I did not, he continued :

" In 1887 I knew that the end of the Emperor Frederick was rapidly approaching. My computations made before the death of the old Emperor William the First, assured me that the Red Prince, as he was called, would not reign more than twelve weeks. He was crowned with the Iron diadem bearing the 'Eye of Bhudha,' and from my calculations based on the birth-dates of the members of the House of Hohenzollern, I knew Death would claim him. The rest is history.

" But when I saw that in due course the young William would also place that fatal diadem on his head I was moved to protest. The birth date of the Prince showed all too clearly that for him, should he invite the curse of the jewel, there would be no swift death, but lingering disaster, with dishonour in the end branded upon his brow. I therefore addressed a memorandum to the young Emperor before he succeeded to the throne, pointing out these facts and urging that another diadem should be substituted.

" It was then I realised he could not be warned. He sent for me and loaded me with reproaches. Finally, drawing himself up, he thundered : ' I am the Kaiser. My dynasty must endure for ever! ' I smiled and left him. Shortly afterwards I was told my presence at the Court was not desired."

I pass over much that was of interest told me by this ancient Seer. But finally he begged me to come to Berlin as quickly as I could, so that he might carry out an experiment he had long contemplated. I confess when he whispered it in my ear I hesitated before its daring. Still, exploration in the realms of Occultism and mystery made a call I could not resist. I agreed that, as soon as I could get a few free days, I would come over to Berlin. With a satisfied smile, he wrung my hand and melted gently from my consulting-room.

In a small street turning out of the Friedrichstrasse, Herr Zunklehorn had his abode. It was an ancient house, stuffed with old furniture and darkened by its tiny windows. Up in what had been the attic he had fitted up a library and laboratory. There, huddled pell-mell, were old books, parchments, strange stones gleaming brightly, circles and discs, charts of lives, and many queer objects that I could not fathom.

Upon his own ground, Herr Zunklehorn seemed more imposing than when he had visited me in London. He wore on his head a skull cap made from the fur of a wild cat; his long robe was like that of the old alchemists; if ever a man looked a survival of some ancient mystic it was Zunklehorn.

Presently the door opened and there entered a young woman with a smooth, expressionless face. I was immediately impressed by her extraordinary appearance. It was as though she moved in a hypnotic trance. Gliding round the table, she took a seat in a high carved chair. She did not speak to me or take the slightest notice of my presence.

" This," said Zunklehorn briefly, " is my ' assistant.' Through her I can raise up the spirits of the dead even as Samuel was brought up by the Witch of Endor." He paused, and continued impressively :

" My dear Cheiro, you know something, I doubt not, of the power of incantations carried out under proper conditions. My time is short. But all is now in readiness for my Grand Experiment."

He then pushed back the table, drew a circle in chalk upon the floor, took in hand a sacred talisman engraved with a mystic number, and uttered the incantatory chant. The girl sat erect in her chair, seemingly indifferent to all that was passing.

The room was shuttered. Gradually the little light filtered away until it became so dark I could hardly see.

The muttering of the incantation continued. Suddenly the girl uttered a loud, rending cry that startled me. She rocked from side to side, holding herself as if in mortal pain. Now a stream of greenish light appeared in a far corner of the room. It was a pillar of luminous light, faintly illuminating the face of the convulsed girl.

The pillar swayed from side to side. Then drew nearer to Herr Zunklehorn. Now I could see it was acquiring human shape, but the head was immense, entirely out of proportion to the outlined body. It was the head of a colossus with the remainder that of an ordinary man.

Suddenly a stream of words poured from the lips of the girl. It was something about

" Lord " and " Master " ; and as she babbled furiously, the swaying pillar grew more human save for the enlarged head.

Zunklehorn ceased his incantations. In a sonorous voice he cried : " Speak, O mighty Soul! Who art thou come from the silent Beyond ? " And through the lips of the writhing medium issued a deep, authoritative voice :

" Frederick, called the Great, King of Prussia and Margrave of Brandenburg. Why callest thou me ? "

I confess a strange thrilling sensation ran through my veins when I now saw the etherial form had shaped more strongly. It was easy to trace the resemblance to the classic picture of Frederick the Great, well known to everybody who has seen the huge portrait in the Berlin National Gallery.

There followed a long interrogation between Zunklehorn and the spirit, the answers being delivered through the entranced medium. I could not easily follow what was said, as the German used was almost archaic, but afterwards Zunklehorn wrote down the gist of it for my benefit.

In brief, it was a solemn warning delivered to Zunklehorn that the Kaiser was rushing on to disaster ; that war would come in August, 1914 ; that the War-lord would be overthrown in 1918 ; that he would go into exile and his dynasty fall in ruins. Finally, his fatal year period was *foreshadowed to begin* in 1918.

Gradually the apparition faded away and the medium regained her fixed calm and glided silently from the room. Zunklehorn then told me that for years he had been working for the propitious moment to bring back the spirit of the great Frederick. "Now," he said somewhat wistfully, "I must quit this mortal state and I shall leave my predictions in your hands."

It is, of course, a matter of history that Herr Zunklehorn died in Berlin during the War, somewhere about 1917. He had previously visited Russia and had been granted an audience of the Czar; for that monarch never lost an opportunity to converse with a mystic. But Rasputin had been jealous of the German's powers and had procured his banishment on the pretext that he was an enemy spy. He died under mysterious circumstances, being found stretched upon the floor of his apartment surrounded by the evidence of his connection with the uncanny.

With regard to the prophecies of woe he uttered concerning the Kaiser, it is notorious that the Eye of Bhudha was an evil gem with a malignant history of ruin behind it.

Raped by a French soldier from a golden statue of Bhudha in a temple in Ceylon, a curse had been uttered by its custodian, an aged priest, who had been struck down by the marauding soldier. For a time it blazed in the turban of Din Nur, the Sultan of Turkey; his favourite wife murdered him for it and in return was made consort of the next Caliph.

Defeated in battle, the gem passed into Holy Tibet, and remained there until a Khurdish warrior stole it from the palace of the Priest-king. It passed into India, stained with blood of many feuds, and finally reached Amsterdam, where it was sold by a merchant to a Jewish diamond dealer.

Passing through Silesia, this dealer was arrested by the police of Frederick the Great. On finding the gem in his baggage, the stone was taken to the king. With swift decision, the monarch hanged the merchant and appropriated the stone. Before he died, the Jew breathed anew the curse, and with prophetic vision announced that in due course the wearer of the gem should be an outcast, driven from his palace, and destined to be the last reigning monarch of the Hohenzollerns. History shows how the spell of the evil gem has worked upon the fortunes of the Kaiser.

I may here remark that the German people are keenly interested in Occultism and the Supernatural. Their legends are saturated with evidences of the belief in mysterious occurrences and the workings of Fate.

Although I never actually had a season in Berlin devoted to receiving clients, I have been brought into contact with many men and women who were closely connected with the old Court that passed away at the end of the Great War. While in London many of them would visit me, and I recall many interesting experiences.

Among them was Count Stefel, at one time close friend of the now fallen Kaiser and in pre-war days a man of immense wealth. He visited me and in conversation mentioned the existence of a family apparition that appeared immediately before the death of the head of his house. It took the form of a grotesque little hunchback, and in this may be traced the well-known German story of Rumpelstiltzchen, the mischievous imp who brought disaster upon those who neglected the observance of occult rites.

The Count told me that his father was dressing for dinner one evening in his old castle on the Rhine, when he thought he heard a tapping on the casement of the window. He pulled aside the blind and there, astride a tree bough that was close, was the boding form of the death-warning. He wrote down the fact on a piece of paper, sealed it and put the envelope in a drawer. The next day, while out driving, the horses bolted, the carriage overturned, and the Count was killed. After the funeral the letter was discovered.

Count Stefel questioned me closely concerning these warning forms that haunt certain families. There is indeed no explanation; they are mysterious harbingers of death, and that is all that can be said. At his request I cast a horoscope for him. I saw that forty-four was plainly his fatal number ; he pooh-poohed the idea, however, and said he would live to be eighty. He was then in his forty-third year.

It was on the eve of the outbreak of war. Many Britishers were hurrying home to get out of Germany before the storm burst. A dear friend of mine, who was a great lover of Germany and particularly of exploring the Rhine, got back by the skin of his teeth. Chatting over the circumstance with me, he happened to say :

" I received great kindness and hospitality from Stefel, who is, I believe, known to you. I did not stay at his castle, but at the inn close by. On the morning I departed there was a terrible commotion. The Count had been found dead in his bedroom, seated in his chair, with a sheet of writing paper in front of him, on which was scribbled 44." Why he wrote that figure on that particular occasion will never be known; all I can say is that he had reached the fatal age of forty-four, which I had told him would mark his last milestone.

" All who admit of the existence of Destiny will see nothing more than natural in the fact—that she indicates the way at each turning of the road."

DR. ARNALDO CERVESATO.

CHAPTER IX

A WEB OF MYSTERY IN A CHINESE " CAVE OF DEVILS "

In London I was visited by the Marquis Ito, the famous Japanese statesman and War Minister. There was a remarkable sequel when, in after years, I went to Tokyo and China. A Chinese Mystic whose incantations and spells conjured up Visions of the Future. The tragic end of the Marquis Ito foreshadowed by one of these scenes.

I HAVE always felt a strong interest in the Japanese and Chinese races, knowing both to be deeply impregnated with Magic and Mystery. Some of their Wise Men have deeply studied Occultism and have a profound knowledge of the effect of planetary influences upon the human race.

It was therefore with considerable interest I welcomed, one afternoon in my consulting-room in London, a very cultured Japanese gentleman who had come to me on the recommendation of Mara Tschpw, a Japanese scholar who wrote a book on Western civilisation that aroused much controversy.

My visitor showed considerable knowledge of Occultism, and particularly desired me to explain to him something of my science of numbers, whereby events can be predicted.

In working out the past events of his life,
I told him that, although born of parents in
a high social standing in Japan. he had adopted a life of extraordinary adventure—had
been a sailor, and visited many countries for
the purpose of studying Western civilisation,
and that at the present moment he was playing a part in some secret negotiations of great
importance to his native land. As to the
future, I predicted for him a brilliant zenith
of high position and power, when he would
be honoured as one of the greatest men of his
country.

It was significant, however, that the end
was marked with unmistakable suddenness
and violence. I warned him of this as plainly
as I could. He shrugged his shoulders and
said with Oriental fatalism: "This has already
been predicted. Can you give me any idea of
the year?"

I made a calculation and said : " So far as
I can say, 1909 will be the year of danger and
particularly the latter part." He made a
careful note of this. He then said :

" It is very interesting to find that what
you have told me concerning my early life is
absolutely correct. Here is my card."

I found my visitor was the Marquis Horo-
bumi Ito, who shortly afterwards became
Foreign Minister for Japan and War
Minister.

He told me how in his early life, though
born, as I had said, of a noble family, he

determined to study Western civilisation. To leave his country for " the land of the foreign devils " was treason, punishable with death ; he therefore shipped as a sailor before the mast and came to England.

Here he lived in obscurity for several years, studying English customs and government from every angle. When he returned he was able to convince the Elder Statesmen that the only path for Japan was progress along Western lines, taking as the model Great Britain and her institutions.

This aroused terrible opposition from the Old Nobility and for a time he was in danger of his life. While pursued by soldiers through Tokyo a Japanese lady hid him beneath the floor of a native teashop. That lady lived to become the wife of the Prince Ito, which title he was given by his grateful country later on in his life.

After a most interesting discussion, he said : " You really ought to visit China and Japan, Cheiro ; there would be so much there to interest you. If you are ever in Tokyo do not fail to call on me."

At the time, the idea of a visit to the Far East seemed out of the question. I was daily turning away dozens of would-be clients and had promised to go back to the United States for an important lecture tour.

However, Fate stepped in ; I was thrown into contact with a financier of world-wide reputation who was interested in certain delicate concession negotiations in Japan and China. He was unable to go himself and suggested I should take his place; thinking that a combined holiday and business trip would prove beneficial, I consented.

After a pleasant voyage I found myself in Tokyo. I soon left my card at the palace of the Marquis. He sent and asked me to call; but he could not devote so much time to me as he wished, as the China-Japanese dispute was rapidly coming to a head and the War Office was seething with activity.

I dined with him twice, the first time being entertained in true Japanese style, the second in European fashion, when even the servants spoke perfect English.

Owing to the disturbed outlook I found it necessary to hurry to Lu Shun K'ou, now famous as Port Arthur,* at that time a Chinese possession, very poorly fortified, situated at the extreme south of the Peninsula of Liao-tung, in the Chinese Principality of Manchuria. Here I had to meet several of the prominent War Lords to negotiate with them certain concessions.

On my arrival all was the wildest confusion. War had been declared and it was the admitted intention of the Japanese to march a big army down through Manchuria to take the Port. In his capacity of War Minister, the Marquis Ito went with the troops who,

---

* First taken by the Japanese in 1894, leased to Russia, surrendered to Japan January 1st, 1905.

for the first time, were going to put into
practice their Western training in warfare.

As far as my business was concerned, with
Eastern lassitude, nothing developed for some
time. The Chinese demanded so much
"palm oil" that I had to seek fresh instructions from my friend in London. In
the meantime, anxious to learn more of that
wonderful part of Manchuria, I made an
excursion far into the country.

By means of relays of wiry ponies, I
travelled some hundred miles into this
Principality, over mountains and rivers,
with glimpses every now and again of queer
villages and lordly Chinese palaces.

On one of these excursions I came to a
splendid house situated on the side of a
mountain. The slopes around had been ter-
raced into enchanted gardens; just at the
foot of these gardens ran the main road leading down from the north to Port Arthur.

While I was admiring this almost fairy-like
palace, a train of Chinese servants in brilliant
coloured tunics emerged from the gates, bearing a palanquin upon rods of bamboo. From
the fact that the servants had the dragon in
gold embroidered upon their breasts, I knew
their master must be a Chinese of the highest
rank and a connection of The Son of Heaven,
as the Chinese Ruler was called.

To my surprise, however, the bearers
stopped, and presently their headman came
to me, and inclining his head on his breast,

indicated that the Chinese gentleman in the palanquin would like to speak to me.

Going to the side of the gorgeously lacquered conveyance, I saw sitting inside a noble-looking Celestial in full native dress. Inclining his head courteously, he addressed me in perfect English (for, as I afterwards learned, he had travelled extensively and was not unacquainted with London).

" Wilt thou be pleased, O honourable One," he said, " to stop a little time and partake of my wretched and poor hospitality in my mean house ? "

The style, of course, was the acme of Chinese politeness, that demands a depreciation of everything possessed by the giver of hospitality. I accepted, and in a very short time I was being conducted by a ceremonious gathering of servants into the mysterious loveliness of the perfect Chinese dwelling-place of a man of rank. For my new-found friend I found out afterwards was a Mandarin, and a governor of the district.

After I had bathed and refreshed myself with tea, the Mandarin showed me some of the wonders of his house. The latter was four-square* and in the centre was a huge

* Everything to do with the figure 4 or its symbol, a square, is regarded as full of occult meaning in China. The first division of mankind in China was fourfold. The fields and lands were divided into 4 parts, which division is still retained. The Chinese provinces were subdivided into 4 classes. Most of the Chinese cities originally were in the form of a square, divided into 4 parts by two cross-streets running to the 4 Cardinal points. The " Forbidden City," the inner part of Peking, is in the form of a square, and the famous Altar

courtyard, where a fountain played. Round this courtyard on the ground floor were various rooms, each decorated in a different style. The Hall of Welcome, where the Mandarin received his guests; the Chamber of Sweet Rest, a dream room in tender shades; the Apartment of Exquisite Pleasure, where meals were served; the Abode of Wisdom, where he received his chosen friends and conversed with them. Higher up were the sleeping chambers.

I sat down that night to a Chinese dinner that was the last word in the Celestial art of cookery. At times I was in doubt as to the precise nature of the little dishes that came and went, but there was no question as to their delicious flavour. Right through the dinner, hidden native singers sang their sweet melodies, while there was a ground-swell of deeper harmony from the native drum and Chinese oboe. It was indeed a night to be remembered in the Flowery Land.

Afterwards, in the Abode of Wisdom, the Mandarin conversed with me. First he was anxious to have the latest news from Port Arthur, for the coming war with the Japanese engrossed all thoughts. "They are devils," he said simply. "And must be exterminated."

Later, the conversation turned on Magic and Mystery; he had in some unaccountable

of Earth is a square. In the ancient Chinese book, *Lun-Yü*, Part X, chap. viii, it is stated that "Confucius did not eat anything that was not cut square, for the princely man did not leave off correctness even being in haste."

way heard of my work in London, he knew of my arrival in Manchuria, and hence came out to meet me as I passed near his palace.

The next morning I was aroused by a most dismal howling, as if a herd of wild dogs were giving tongue. Descending, I was met in the main hall by the head servant, who conducted me into the courtyard. There, sitting beneath a cherry tree, sat the Mandarin. Around him howled and wailed a score of his wives.

Amazed by the scene, I pressed forward and demanded to know the cause of the trouble.

"Most honourable stranger," he said, "it was written upon the tablets by the Wise Confucius that No Man Knoweth what the Morrow will Bring! Alas, I am undone! The house wherein burns the sacred light on the shrine of my ancestors is to be defiled by the Japanese Devils. All will be in ruins before the sun sinks to-morrow. Let me die, rather than see the desolation of my house and my gardens and my pleasant places."

The Mandarin continued in this strain for some time. At last I was able, by close questioning, to ascertain the cause of his doleful distress.

It seemed that at dawn a Chinese runner had come in to announce that the Japanese army was in full march upon Port Arthur and must pass of necessity down the great road on the verge of his estate.

Judging the Japanese by his own country's army, he could see nothing but utter desolation as the "devils" swarmed over the country. The looting of his house and the destruction of his farms and gardens was to him a foregone conclusion, but worse than all, the desecration of the shrines of his ancestors.

I endeavoured to comfort him, while the wailing and howling continued without intermission. At length the Mandarin arose and with a dignified bow, said:

"Most honourable stranger! Who am I, mere dust, that I should parade my empty grief before you, or that my wives should howl as the baboons in the cane brakes?" With a gesture of resignation, he signed to his wailing women to seek their quarters while he prepared to offer prayers to Bhudha.

It was at that moment there came to me what I can only describe as an inspiration. I recalled that the Marquis Ito was with the Japanese army now marching towards Port Arthur. That the troops must pass on the road through the estate was obvious.

Staying the departure of the Mandarin, I said:

"Weep not before there is cause. Give me writing tablets and a swift messenger. I will stay the disaster that threatens to sweep away thy possessions."

"Thou dost jest, O honourable stranger,

to assuage the lamentations of a sublime fool," he replied mournfully.

For reply I hastily scribbled a note addressed to the Marquis, briefly detailing the circumstances, and asking that, for the hospitality I had received from the Mandarin, his house and possessions might be spared.

While my Chinese friends watched with amazed suspense, I dispatched a messenger with strict instructions that he should seek the Japanese headquarters and place the note in the hands of the all-powerful War Minister.

The day was passed in anxious waiting. At sundown the jaded messenger returned with a letter. It announced in cordial terms that the Marquis Ito would respect my request and that strictest orders had been given that there should be no looting by troops when passing the estates of the Mandarin.

Through that night and all the next day the tide of the Japanese troops flowed down the road. Not one single case of interference or looting was reported; and finally the Marquis and his staff rode by, drawing rein to have a short conversation with myself before he dashed onwards to Port Arthur.

I need hardly record that the gratitude of the Mandarin was only equalled by his amazement that I should possess such influence. To him it indicated almost supernatural qualities, and he admitted that the moment he had known of my arrival at Port Arthur he had determined to meet me.

After meditating in silence for some time, he turned and said:

"O Honourable One, my poor gratitude for what thou hast done is as the grain of dust compared to the Mountains of Cho-foa. But if you will allow me, through another, to unlock the door of Hidden Mysteries, I will show thee what no Foreign Devil—thy pardon, O Stranger, for the name I must give thee —has ever been permitted to see—and live!"

Thus it came about, through the overflowing gratitude of the Mandarin, I was given some insight into the amazing mysteries of Chinese Occultism, the secrets of which are most jealously guarded from foreigners.

The next day we were conveyed in two palanquins some eight miles over another mountain. We stopped outside a small Bhudhist temple, served by several priests called *bonzes*. My host was a Bhudhist and a great patron of this temple.

Putting off our shoes and arraying myself in a peculiar mantle of dark blue, covered with the Chinese version of the signs of the Zodiac, we entered the temple, while our servants remained reverently outside. Inside the small building it was almost dark. A single light burned before a shrine which contained a golden statue of Bhudha. The priests and my host prostrated themselves. Then approaching the shrine closely, a rough stone stairway disclosed itself as a heavy door was lifted in the floor of the Temple.

Descending by the aid of lights held by the priests, we found ourselves in a low, crypt-like vault. Passing along a winding passage that I noted gradually descended deeper into the bowels of the earth, we came at length to a place where the roof lifted. As my eyes grew accustomed to the gloom, I could see that I was in a subterranean grotto. On one side, at a few feet from the ground, was a small hole in the living rock. I peeped through ; to my amazement I could see down the immense mountain into the dizzy depths of the valley beneath. The grotto was, in fact, in the side of the shoulder of the mountain.

The attendant priests retired. The Mandarin remained immobile. Then, while I peered impatiently around, there emerged from one end of the grotto, coming forth from a small recess screened by curtains, a dehuman figure. As It moved forward, the Mandarin, shielding his face with his hands, murmured low :

" Behold, Ta-Theo-Tam, Timeless and Ageless, the Mystic of the Mountains."

The figure was certainly one that fitted with the weird surroundings. The face, carved as in ivory, gave the impression of incredible age and knowledge ; the eyes were glazed, whether blind I did not know. On his head was a wide Tartar hat shaped like an inverted bowl; his spare frame was wrapped in a black silk robe adorned with a skull embroidered in white. Upon his shoulder squatted a huge spotted toad. His hands were concealed in his vest sleeves, but as he halted before us, he suddenly drew out his right hand and in the air described certain mystic circles and signs of a cabalistic significance, that I recognised from some of my previous Occult experiences.

Speaking Chinese, the Mandarin addressed the Mystic. Before replying, he bent and drew round himself a circle on the earth floor, using his long finger-nail for the purpose. The toad hopped from his shoulder, squatting within the line thus drawn, its brilliant eyes gleaming like diamonds. Presently the Ancient rose and spoke slowly. The Mandarin translated :

" The Foreign Devil comes from beyond the seas. He is an Adept in some of the knowledge bequeathed by the gods. He hath much business in hand that will fail. He knoweth something of the Greater Mysteries, but I, Ta-Theo-Tam, Guardian of the secrets of the Wise Ones, will show him my power."

He thrust into my hand a piece of copper, smooth and shining. It seemed to have been at one time a piece of a native shield. Through the Mandarin I was bidden to gaze upon it.

At first I could see nothing. Then gradually, to my amazement, pictures and scenes appeared one after the other, main incidents in my past life shone out clear and distinct, all leading to a definite point to my consulting-room in London. I recognised engravings on the wall, the queer-shaped Indian chair, even the antique bowl it was my foible to have filled with fresh blooms each day before an image of Bhudha which I had always kept on a kind of altar. And while I gazed entranced, I saw myself seated in my usual place. A man entered, and sat in the seat reserved for callers. I had no difficulty in recognising him. It was the Marquis Ito. Even while I stared at it, the scene dissolved and another formed. This time I saw an unfamiliar city with grotesque buildings and tortuous streets. A carriage dashed madly along, with men on galloping horses surrounding it. And as it flashed by I saw a drooping figure supported by two men. The head was bare ; blood flowed down the face ; but I recognised it instantly. It was the Marquis Ito.

And even while I mused on this, there fell upon my ears a harsh, clanging laugh, horrible beyond expression. I glanced into the face of the Mystic. His eyes were now blazing with demoniac fire, his features worked convulsively, and, though not from his lips, howls of devil-laughter filled the room.

I turned mutely to the Mandarin for the explanation, although the picture I had seen form before my eyes foreshadowed the untimely death of the Marquis Ito.

" Ta-Theo-Tam says War-maker Devil Ito

shall die by hand of Korean brother. He says gods very pleased."

But now the Mystic commenced to shuffle upon his feet and broke out into a capering dance. The toad hopped in rude harmony with the slippered feet. A thick gloom seemed to oppress the cave; a stifling sensation oppressed me. The walls began to recede. I was conscious of great space and height. The Mystic appeared elevated, a monstrous figure standing upon a carved pillar. All around him danced devilish figures in Chinese dress, while the clanging of a great gong sounded with maddening insistence. It was indeed a vision of Hell, the distorted faces of the dancers, excited to frenzy by their incantatory chant, filling me with a sensation of terror.

Gradually the scene faded. I felt a current of fresh air, and opened my eyes. I was lying upon the ground. The Mandarin was bending over me with solicitude, holding a cup of water to my lips.

" Where am I ? " I asked feebly. " Those horrors I saw——"

" Think not upon them, Honourable One," returned the Mandarin. " Come let us return to my house and eat and drink in happiness. So let the dark visions of the cave be forgotten! "

It is, of course, a matter of history that on October 26th, 1909, Prince Ito (for he was raised to this rank for his services to Japan) was assassinated at Harbin by a Korean assailant. It was proved that the murderer belonged to the famous Ha-Ha-Wei Tong—a secret society who had sworn death to all Japanese responsible for the victory of that country over China. The loss of Port Arthur was avenged, but, as is well known, it was a barren victory for Japan. Great Britain, France and Russia slipped in, and Japan was compelled to give up the rich prize she had so deservedly won, and lease Port Arthur to Russia. Through the skilful diplomacy of Prince Ito, Japan strengthened her position by the alliance with Great Britain, until finally, at a terrible expenditure of blood and treasure, she wrested Port Arthur from the Russians and established herself firmly in Manchuria and Korea.

But in the process Prince Ito was the sacrifice. I have often wondered what devilish spell was put upon him by Ta-Theo-Tam, the Mystic of the Cave of Devils.

CHAPTER X

I MEET A " RECLUSE " IN LONDON AND PASS THROUGH A SEVERE ORDEAL

THERE WAS LIVING IN LONDON A STRANGE RECLUSE WHO DESIRED TO SEE ME. AS A RESULT HE PUT ME THROUGH A SEVERE TEST THAT WAS SUCCESSFULLY PASSED. A CLOSE INTIMACY RESULTED, AND THE RECLUSE CONFIDED SOME OF HIS AMBITIONS CONNECTED WITH RESEARCHES IN OCCULTISM WITH EXTRAORDINARY RESULTS.

IS there a connection between music and communion with the dead?

This fascinating question has long occupied my mind. In it lies, I have no doubt, the key to unlock the realm of psychic intercourse, and the feeblest imagination can visualise the possibilities.

How I was led to an investigation of this question makes up one of the most romantic episodes of my career, which I now propose to publish for the first time.

When I returned from my first American tour I found many hundreds of impatient people who were anxious to consult me. I had created a *furore* in New York and throughout the United States, and I found even greater interest in my work awaiting me in London.

201

One day I received a visit from a young
Parsee named Jehangier Colah. Ostensibly
he was studying medicine in London, but I
quickly discovered his real interest lay in
Mysticism and matters pertaining to the
Occult. He was especially interested in tele-
pathy and thought-transference, and many
were the fascinating experiments we worked
out together.

On several occasions he spoke guardedly
of a remarkable character living in London.
I gathered he was a recluse, and my attention
was stimulated when Jehangier let fall certain
hints that this man was in reality a Mystic
of the highest order.

One day Jehangier said he had a message
for me from the recluse, who desired to see
me. The possibility of an interesting experience excited me and I gladly assented.
All I knew was that his residence was somewhere in Hampstead.

The name of the man I did not know. My
Parsee friend would not reveal it and before
we started, bound me with a solemn oath not
to attempt to find out the identity of the
recluse unless he gave me permission to do so.

London is full of extraordinary people. I
had already passed through many strange
experiences; for the career I had adopted
brought me into contact with all sorts and
conditions of people, while confidences of an
unusual kind were often poured into my ears.

That evening we travelled up to Hampstead and in due course arrived at the house of the Unknown. It was a fine old isolated mansion on the edge of the Heath, with a magnificent view over London, stretching away in the far distance. Embowered in trees, it pleased my fancy to think that it was an ideal retreat for a Man of Mystery.

Jehangier left me in the hall for a few moments, and I had time to glance around. Exquisite paintings adorned the walls, and some very beautiful pieces of statuary and bronze stood on the huge mantelpiece. All bore evidence to a man of taste and deep culture.

After a short absence, Jehangier returned and together we went up the richly carpeted staircase to a magnificent set of rooms that occupied the whole of the first floor.

Pushing aside some heavy dark purple curtains, we entered a fine *salon*, exquisitely furnished. Then passing through a smaller room, we came to another. To my surprise it contained an organ so large that it occupied the whole of one side of the room. In a window recess overlooking the garden there stood a grand piano and an unusually beautiful harp.

Awaiting me was a medium-sized, but noble-looking individual. His high-domed head and piercing eyes proclaimed the man of intellect and conscious power; his quiet voice, though slightly foreign in accent, impressed me as belonging to one accustomed to being obeyed. His deep purple coat, flowing cravat of lighter hue, and ring that gleamed upon the forefinger of his slender left hand gave him a touch of the *bizarre*.

He surveyed me deliberately for some seconds.

" Well, Cheiro," he said at length, " I have heard much of you and am pleased to meet you. But I must be frank. As to your pretensions—for mark you, sir, to me they are but pretensions until I have had satisfying proof—I shall propose a test of your powers which I trust you will not refuse to undergo."

I bowed. Jehangier left us together and the conversation took a more intimate tone.

I observed for the first time that he was lame and walked with a stick. But one did not think of this deformity in the presence of his dominating personality. His grand head and face reminded me of pictures of some Roman emperor.

" Who is this mysterious person ? " I wondered. There was evidence of wealth around him and the " unusual " was stamped upon his features, dress and bearing. My thoughts were interrupted by the recluse saying abruptly :

" I sent for you to give me personally a test of your powers. There are many charlatans and frauds about who pretend to deal in occult knowledge. They are not the custodians of the sacred wisdom only derived by tireless study and by the possession of a natural clairvoyance." He paused and then went on in a softer tone :

" I want you to convince me you have deserved the reputation you have gained, so that I may report of you to some of the mystics I am accustomed to meet in my world-wide travels. First, read my past from the lines of my hands ; if you fail to convince me of your gifts, you shall go as you came, and your expenditure of time and trouble will be the only items you need regret."

I bowed assent. We sat down together at a small table by the window.

" One moment," he said, as I commenced to examine the lines of his finely shaped hands. " If you are successful, Cheiro, I will do what I only do for a small circle of trusted friends : I will unveil my identity— until then I am ' The Recluse,' " and he gave a somewhat bitter laugh.

I was nervous, but, as I have stated before, a highly strung condition is always best in obtaining good results.

In this curious case, as I looked at his hands, scenes of past events seemed to form with startling clearness. My trained clairvoyant brain saw a series of pictures forming one after the other of his past life. I talked rapidly, fearing to miss what I saw.

" At the age of fifteen you were hailed as a musical prodigy." I went on : " Sheets of music seemed to flow from your fingers as if by magic. Now I see you later on as the centre of observation in a great hall thronged with people. You are being presented with a gold medal inscribed with the name of a musician whose fame became world-wide."

" Can you give the name ? " he demanded.

I spelt out the name " Gounod."

" Strange," he said musingly, half withdrawing his hands, " but that is singularly correct. At the age of fifteen I was presented with the gold medal for music by the Conservatoire of Paris. Gounod and myself gained equal honours and both our names appeared on the same medal. Proceed."

" For some reason which I cannot explain you gave up following music as a profession. I see you now robed as a French *advocate*. You are pleading before a Court. The prisoner in the dock is dressed in the uniform of the French Navy. There is an acquittal and the man leaves the dock and comes impulsively to you to shake your hand and kisses you upon each cheek. It is an hour of triumph."

" Yes, Cheiro, that was indeed a triumph. I gave up my music and studied law that I might gain that man his liberty. For a long time he had lain under a false accusation of promoting mutiny in the Navy and had been banished to a penal settlement. There was a reason why I toiled so hard for him.

" His mother had one day, when I passed her cottage, given me a glass of milk when I asked for water. I saw she was suffering great anxiety of mind. I heard from her that her only son had been falsely accused of promoting mutiny in the Navy and had been sent for life to Devil's Island. I studied to become an *advocate*, I fought his case in every French Court, and finally in the Cour de Cassation I obtained his liberty."

" At thirty years of age," I continued, " a great love entered your life, you gave up everything for the woman you adored, and when she died you entered a monastery. I see a library heaped with books—long years of study—a return into the world of men with some purpose for which you now work night and day."

" You are right," he muttered, and drew away his hands as if the reincarnation of his career hurt him beyond endurance.

" Cheiro, you have indeed unveiled the Past, and—yes, I confess it!—I dread that you should tell me the Future that awaits me. Some day, perhaps, but not now. You have triumphantly passed the test. I ask no more ; from now on we shall be brothers in the study of the profound mysteries of life and death."

He took a limping turn up and down the apartment, as though memories of the past haunted him. Then coming to me, and drawing himself to his full height, he said slowly :

" I must now tell you who I am. I am the Duc de Ravigo, the last of my race. One

time I was a musical prodigy of France and
friend of great musicians; but now content
to be known by my mother's name, as
Edmond Savory D'Odiardi, Occultist, Mystic
and Physician. One of my ancestors received
the title of Duke on the field of Austerlitz from
Napoleon the First. His name may be read
to-day carved on the roll of honour on the
Arc de Triomphe."

As he uttered these words there was something almost awe-inspiring in his appearance.
I recalled the many stories I had heard from
the older generation in Paris of a marvellous
boy who had great musical genius; how
he had abandoned music and had become
a brilliant *advocate* at the French Bar. Suddenly he had disappeared from the haunts of
men and, as usual, a woman was said to be
at the bottom of the mystery.

How little I had thought on keeping the
appointment that night that I was to be fated
to meet one of the most remarkable men of the
century.

Presently he said:

"As you have passed through the test I
set for you, I will put another proposition
before you. But first I will play some music
in order to ascertain the vibrations that will
unite our spirits in one harmonious bond and
enable us to solve problems of interest to us
both."

I have heard great music played on many
occasions in my life, but never such as I

listened to that evening. He seemed to play the story of his life—the success, the triumph ; and then the romance that led to a cloistered life. Through it all whispered the tones of the Angelus, calling and pleading, and growing fainter as the years rolled on.

The last rays of the sun shone through the window of the salon ; the shadows of night crept in and darkened the room. Still the figure at the organ played on. Suddenly I heard another sound, so faint at first that I caught my breath to listen. A whispering sound *seemed to pass over the strings of the harp;* it grew louder, until harp and organ joined in unison, finally dying away in silence.

I seemed to awake from a dream. The "recluse" stood before me with shining eyes.

" Cheiro," he whispered, " you heard *her.* She used always to play that harp for me, *and she does so still !* " He paused and then coming close, whispered in my ear : " I am groping after the great secret and you must help me. To bring back the dead from ' the Beyond ' *as and when I will them to come.* That is my life's work. I have sent for you because you can help me. I have proved to-night that your magnetic vibrations are in tune with my own and your clairvoyant mind can be of the greatest assistance to me. I will now put before you the proposition I hinted at before."

He then went on to tell me of his daring

experiments to commune with the dead. " If you will agree to help me," he continued, " you will never regret your decision."

I agreed and gave him my hand to seal the compact.

He then explained that he believed the law of vibration was the key to unlock the secrets of " the Beyond."

" Our life here," he said, " has a vibration of its own; *the ' life beyond ' has another.* When the two are made to harmonise the veil is lifted between the two planes, and spirits are able to make themselves manifest."

We talked on till nearly morning. I left bewildered, but filled with a desire to know more of this remarkable character who had buried himself away from men as though he were already in the grave. It was not long before I was summoned again to see him.

I pass over as a sacred experience the evenings when he did indeed, through the thrilling harmonies of music, bring the spirit of the woman he had loved back from the shadows of " the Beyond." But I soon found that beneath this tenderness and sentiment he was not satisfied: he had got so far, but he was determined to go farther, to launch out upon the boundless sea of experiments that I must confess took my breath away, while at the same time they thrilled me with their daring.

One evening he said :

" In my investigations I have discovered

certain chords of music that create the class of vibration necessary for the manifestation of still higher beings who inhabit what is miscalled the ' invisible world.' I can now draw some of these great spirits at will at any hour of the day or night."

" Wonderful," I murmured.

" Wonderful! " he agreed, while a strange light illuminated his eyes. " *But I am not satisfied.* I must do better! "

It was then that this extraordinary man put a startling proposition before me.

" Cheiro," he said, " I have been waiting for years to meet a man like you. I want to continue experiments I have been making for a long time in getting messages from a still higher plane—the plane whose occult vibrations control the destiny of the planet on which we live. If you will agree to join me in these researches, you will never, I think, regret your decision."

I did not hesitate.

" My theory is, as I have told you," he went on, " that the law of vibration is the secret of ' the veil between.' "

" In other words," he continued, " mediums who produce the phenomenon known as ' the materialisation ' of spirits have a peculiar vibration of their own, and by their very presence conditions are created which enable this phenomenon to be produced. In my investigations I have discovered that certain chords create the class of vibration necessary for still more important manifestations, and so I am able at will to draw some of these higher beings to me. In my case, however, I am not yet satisfied with the results that might satisfy most investigators. My ambition is to come in contact with the great spirits of the past, the great Teachers who had a direct mission to humanity, and who can still teach us the mysteries of design and purpose which is the real secret of existence.

"In such experiments I must have your co-operation ; a helper who can translate the words and symbolism of other ages into our own."

He paused and I waited expectantly.

"I will give you just one example of what I mean," he continued. "The music you heard to-night produces on every occasion the spirit of the woman I loved. When she is here I have no need for an interpreter, every chord finds a corresponding one in my being and we talk to one another in music as human beings converse in speech.

"This, however, does not satisfy my desires. Love is not what life was created for— love is but the companion of our pilgrimage, lest the loneliness of life should seem too great.

"For fear you think me but a vain dreamer, I will explain later to you some of the experiments I have pursued for quite a number of years. Although I am far from being able to explain the reason, I am conscious that nothing takes place by chance. That the faintest chord of harmony produces its counter wave in endless space until like two affinities *they blend together and reappear* in greater strength. Let us meet again to-morrow, and I will put before you a mystery that may well stagger reason, which goes far to prove what mere puppets we are in the plan of that Divine Design, that employs Time and Eternity for its purpose and men and women as co-helpers in the execution of its plans."

" *All wish to know, but few the price will pay.*"

Juvenal.

" *If the time could arrive when all was known, when there could not be a new investigation or experiment, our keenest pleasure would be at an end. We may, therefore, feel happy in the thought of how much is still unknown.*"

A. C. Vernon Harcourt.

CHAPTER XI

TURNING BACK THE CLOCK OF TIME. PAST AGES RECREATED

Scenes of History lived again. The Panorama of Life and "the Great Secret"

I WAS surprised on arriving the following evening to find that "the Mystic," as I called him in my own mind, had made unusual preparations for the experiment he had planned to carry out.

I had known from the first that he had mastered the most difficult problems of what may be called " etheric electric waves," and long before broadcasting receivers had been thought of, he had fitted up in his house a receptacle that collected both sound and speech from the ether, far beyond anything we have at the present day.

As he had a horror of commercialising his inventions, he had refused all offers of money to place any of his ideas on the market, or to bring them before the notice of the public.

At the risk of digressing from my principal theme in these pages, I feel it is only just to my readers that they may be able to grasp the extraordinary character of the man I am

215

writing about, to turn aside for a moment
and speak of some medical experiments he
carried out with electricity which are known
to other persons in London as well as myself.*

I will only relate a few of these cases as it
would take a volume in itself to tell one half
of what this man accomplished in his varying
stages of activity.

In the first place, he had progressed
farther in a branch of medical electricity
known as the " ionisation of metals " than
perhaps any other man who has lived before
him.

With him he so controlled electric forces
that he was able not only to dissolve any
metal, but he could direct the " ions " of the
dissolving metal into any organ or part of
the body that he so desired.

He knew to his finger-tips the effect that
the " ions of gold " must produce on various
parts of the spinal column and so cured many
of the worst cases of paralysis. In the
same way he caused electric currents to carry
" ions " of copper, silver, or mercury into the
body and so isolated them that they were
only allowed to affect the organ or part under
treatment.

In many cases he cured cancer where an
operation would not have been possible, but
the most outstanding instance of his many
remarkable cures that I came directly in

* This statement is corroborated by an article which appeared in
the *Sunday Times* of February 21st, 1897.

contact with was that of a woman who had the unusual malady called " the blood sweat." It is said that there are only three instances known in the history of medicine, and *this woman was one of them.**

This terrible disease causes the blood to ooze out of the skin all over the body, the result is a slow wasting away of the vitality, until death, after many years, releases the unhappy victim.

It took nearly six months to make a complete cure of the case I am speaking about, but the extreme ends of the fingers resisted all efforts to stop the oozing out of the blood in the most obstinate way. Finally, the patience of this man triumphed, every finger was cured but the third of the left hand. This, there is no question, would have been conquered also, but one day the woman annoyed him by an act of meanness to one of his nurses.

" Madam," the old man said, " God has been good to you. He has, through me, effected your cure. He, like me, abhors meanness—therefore—go *and keep your bloody finger with you for the rest of your life.*"

One of the extraordinary inventions this man made was exhibited to the members of the Academie des Sciences and the account of this invention is among their records in Paris.   This was no less than an instrument

* The full account of this extraordinary case has been placed before me.—ED

called a " Register of Thought "—briefly, the
delicately poised needle in this wonderfully
constructed instrument was affected by the
aura or soul radiation of any person standing
within a few feet of it and recorded by its
movements the effect of thoughts passing
through the brain, such as love, anger, fear,
ambition, and so on. It showed whether a
person had will power, or concentration, or
the reverse, and one of the most remarkable
things about it was that it instantaneously
registered the effects of drugs or alcohol
on the effort of thought.

I personally showed one of these instruments that this man constructed specially for
me to Mr. Gladstone on the occasion of his
inviting me to discuss occult subjects with
him at Hawarden Castle in August, 1897.
England's " Grand Old Man " spent a considerable time with me testing this instrument in a number of ways. I brought away
from this interview a record made by it of
Mr. Gladstone's remarkable power of concentration, which I have still in my possession.

After having in some slight way given my
readers an idea of the many-sided mentality
of the man who is the subject of these pages,
I will now go back to where I digressed, at
the preparations I noticed " the Mystic " had
made for the great experiment he had looked
forward to for so long.

As this is not a scientific work on the subject of " etheric waves," it would be out of

place in these pages to do more than give a general outline of the " apparatus " that had been constructed for this occasion. I will, therefore, only allude briefly to the more salient parts that stood out distinctly from other sections that were more or less invisible.

In the first place it had been known to me for some time that in his medical experiments this remarkable man employed electric earth currents, which, although giving in the ordinary way—as persons interested in such things can easily demonstrate for themselves—about one and a half volts of electricity, were magnified and increased by an apparatus constructed by him to give a voltage of a very considerable amount. By another invention he utilised the electricity in the higher atmosphere, and collected it by storage batteries of enormous dimensions, and these, connected with vacuum glass tubes filled with " neon " or some other gas, produced a light that appeared to flood every part of a room in which one of these lamps was placed.

As a demonstration of the theory that the Law of Vibration was the key by which he could utilise some of the great forces of Nature, he could at any moment, by a chord of music on the organ, piano or harp, call whatever lamp he wished into action, or extinguish any or all of them in a similar manner.

As is well known to all students of science,

it is only the vibration and speed of the revolving molecules that hold the particles of iron, stone or any other solid mass in a state of solidity. This man in his work had demonstrated that human life itself was only a matter of vibration, that when the natural note of vibration sunk below par, the person became what doctors describe as "out of tone" or "under par," although few of the medical men who use these expressions know that in using them they are expressing one of the greatest secrets of human existence.

Following on these lines, this great thinker had evolved the means of *altering the speed, tone or quality* of the vibrations of any human being.

Without causing death, he was able at will to slow down life's responsive throb to such an extent that the sub-conscious brain found its freedom—or it may be that the soul or spirit side of existence was allowed to leave the body for a certain time.

He had on various occasions practised this experiment on myself with remarkable results, but when I noticed some of the apparatus that were now brought together for the great experiment on this particular night, I knew without asking that he had designed some special rôle for me to take.

Some of the arrangements I took in at a glance. Near the window a curious-looking couch covered with copper, insulated with glass feet, attracted my attention. At the head of it lay a compass showing by the position of the needle that the couch lay north to south in a direct line with the magnetic current.

On a table at the side I noticed a helmet of copper with a copper band so constructed to go down the spine, with two arms from it to go round the body and terminate in a twelve-pointed magnet on the solar plexus. Connected to the centre of the helmet an insulated covered wire led through the open windows to a series of copper wires hanging from the edge of the high roof to a few feet from the ground. These in their turn were joined to an aerial of immense height over the house. I further observed that the copper plate on which my feet would rest was connected with a wire which, passing through what he called " a magnifier " at the other end of the room, terminated in an " earth " zinc pole at the bottom of a well in the garden.

In other words, it was intended that my brain should be *exactly like the receiver in a " wireless set."*

" Is there any danger ? " I could not prevent myself from asking.

" My dear Cheiro, there is danger in every experiment in which one tries to control the forces of nature," the Mystic replied. " In this case the principal danger lies in the state of the outside atmosphere; the slightest electric storm, for example, might pass through your body."

" And then ? " I asked.

Looking at me with a very determined expression, he said :

" My dear friend, we all run risk of death every day ; it is ever present by our side in a hundred forms: many die without apparent reason, many are killed just as cattle are, but in their case, unlike that of the cattle, they do not even make useful food, except for worms.

" With you and I, if death should come in one of these experiments, there would be something noble about it. It would come, when like explorers, we were penetrating into the unknown for the benefit of others.

" You gave me your word of honour to carry out any experiment I wanted to make. If I have judged you right, you are not a man to break your word."

What if an accident did happen, I thought, after all; I have no ties or family responsibilities. I am even the last member of my race—it was one of the many reasons why this strange man, he had told me himself, had selected me to be his helper—besides Death is not so terrible, after all. The Dark Angel had nearly called me once or twice before ; if he does come now, I thought, he will come as an old friend, he will hardly need an introduction.

" All right," I laughed. " I won't funk it, only I would like to know what I may be likely to expect."

" What you may expect ? " he repeated. *" Can any of us know that, in such an excursion into the ' unknown'?* I can only tell you, my dear friend, that if what I am about to undertake succeeds, both you and I will gain more knowledge in a night than we otherwise might do in a lifetime.

" Is not that worth any risk ? "

" Decidedly," I answered. " I am ready."

" Before we proceed," he went on, " I must explain in as few words as possible the general theory of my experiment tonight. You are, of course, aware that the divisions of time as made by man have been made only to suit his own convenience, and have no relation whatever to what Time is in its aspect to Eternity. When man is asked to believe that the Creation of the world took place five or six thousand years ago, and that from a first man and woman, and a garden, the nations of the earth became peopled, it is exactly as if a new-born baby were asked to believe that it could tell, who was the weaver who spun its swaddling clothes.

" Man knows nothing as to his beginning—his purpose—or his end. He knows as little about himself as he does about things Divine. He created a god—because he cannot live without one—but man's god is but man multiplied—until his god has become a monstrosity.

" In terror at the thing he created, man made priests to intercede for him—in their turn they created religions to hide their ignorance—laws to support their pretensions and kings to enforce their rights.

"Kings in their turn created armies to fight for them—paid men to kill other men—joined hands with tyrants for self-protection, and enslaved man still more in the meshes of state-craft and priest-craft.

"In the muddle of it all—man forgot his own creation, forgot he had placed a man-god on the Throne of the Divine, and so lost the first principles of Purpose in the blindness of his own vanity and conceit.

"Behind all, on the scroll of Eternity, with infinite patience, Design etches the pattern that the feet of evolution must follow.

"What does it matter in the great scheme of things if civilisations be lost, or the dust of ages hide the brightness of the stars. What does it matter if pigmy nations destroy other pigmies, if religions set up idols for others to pull down.

"Behind all is the 'Thought-force' that created all—the Purpose of Perfection that moulds all—*the Divine Patience that waits for all.*

"It is with such thoughts, my brother," he added, "that we must approach the experiment that we would make to-night; we humbly ask to lift the veil of the Unknown, to learn if possible a little of the mysteries that surround us, to see if Design left its footsteps through the ages—if Purpose laid its plans from the beginning, if life is immortal, if memory lives for ever in the soul of Eternity.

" You are aware, as well as I am, that science has proved that the light of some of our distant stars commenced its journey to the earth when it was ' without form and void ' and ' when darkness was upon the face of the waters.' That light reached this world, perhaps yesterday, after travelling thousands and thousands of years from some far-off star. What, then, if its photographic beams could be reversed and the scenes of long-past ages could be reconstructed before our eyes. There is nothing lost—there is nothing impossible. Let us make the attempt."

Lying down on the couch, he placed the copper helmet on my head and fastened and made the various connections. Going to the organ he struck a series of chords across the lower manual, the vacuum lamps responded, the lights changed and flooded the room with a pale grey shade like that of a ghostly dawn. Again the tones of the organ vibrated through the room, an appealing sombre chant that had faith, devotion, entreaty in its theme, that rose and fell like a living prayer begging and imploring for an answer.

The music ceased. I could see in the weird grey light the figure of the Mystic leaning over the keys, *waiting and listening*.

A slight vibration came down the aerial

leads, passed through my body and echoed back through the magnifier at the end of the room. At first it was nothing more than a vague sound to which one could hardly give a name. Very softly he touched the organ keys again, and again leaned forward to listen. A trembling chord from the aerial answered—it was something more than an echoing vibration, this time it had life in it, with a peculiar undertone of melody.

The Mystic's eyes gleamed with exaltation. Again the organ pealed, and now it was no longer a sob of entreaty, but a pæan of thankfulness and triumph. He stopped suddenly. I saw a figure gliding through the open windows, the harp was struck, white hands were passing swiftly across the strings, deeper notes of the organ joined in a kind of undertone, then both instruments swelled out into a note of superb unison, the aerial answered—and harmonies such as I could never have imagined echoed and vibrated through the room.

We were, however, only at the beginning of things. One unaccountable manifestation followed another in rapid succession. In the earlier part of the evening, while lying on the couch, I had been particularly struck by the wonderful view from the windows of the lights of London in the far distance; it seemed only a few minutes before that I had especially noticed how clearly I recognised the dome of St. Paul's, but now London, with its myriads of shining roofs and spires of churches, had disappeared.

What was happening ? It was impossible for me to make any surmise. I was not in any trance condition that I knew of—my brain seemed just as active as before.

During the last part of that wonderful music my eyes had been fixed on a far-off star in the distant sky. It seemed unusually brilliant. As I lay and watched it, the fantastic idea came through my mind that it would in some way, perhaps, write some message across the mysterious vault of heaven or some celestial form would descend through its rays, but little did I imagine that a still more mysterious manifestation than anything I could have imagined was already forming by my side.

I had not noticed that the music had ceased and its place had been taken by strange voices that were speaking to me and trying to make me understand. I had forgotten that my brain was in reality part of that wonderful receiving instrument, and that these strange voices were being led through me or attracted to me in some inconceivable way.

Suddenly a deep sonorous voice seemed to come through the atmosphere. I had no idea in what language it spoke, but I had no difficulty in understanding every word.

" Child of Man," the voice said, " I have come to show you the mystery of eternal memory by the reconstruction of visions of the past. You have often pondered over the thought that in ancient ages it is said, ' God talked with men,' and that angels and spirits from higher planes associated with mortals and taught them the secrets of Creation, which otherwise they could not have known.   In the inscrutable wisdom of the Thought Force of Purpose, and the Creator of all Design, the Zodiacal system that controls this earth compels it to alter its axis once in every 25,000 years. At the end of each of these periods of Time called by men ' the Precession of the Equinoxes ' the tilt or inclination of the Poles causes oceans to alter, continents to be swept away, civilisations to be destroyed, and new ones to appear.

" You will shortly see with your own eyes one of those previous civilisations where man attained to a higher knowledge of occult laws and general wisdom than he has done at any period in the earth's present existence.

" The scene you are about to behold is that of the long-lost Atlantis at the 'zenith of its greatest power.*

" Shortly before its destruction as a continent some of the most highly educated of its people, being warned by their occult knowledge of the approaching cataclysm, migrated

* The lost Atlantis was mentioned by Plato. He tells how its tragic history of being overwhelmed by the ocean was first related by Egyptian priests. It was in Atlantis that it is supposed Occultism attained its highest power and passed from there to Egypt and other countries of the earth.

to Egypt; another branch of these people journeyed farther east under a patriarch called Adam, who became the ancestor of a race called Israelites. In this manner the secrets of occult knowledge have been passed on from one age to another, although at times distorted and misused by priests of various creeds.

" You will recognise the foundation and origin of all religions in the scene you are about to behold."

Again wonderful vibrations of music were called into play. This time the tones of the organ mingled with chords that appeared to come from far-distant celestial spheres. Attracted by the aerial they passed through my brain and reissued from the magnifier at the other end of the room with redoubled volume. My spirit seemed to leave my body, while at the same time I remained acutely conscious of everything that was going on around me.

The distant roofs of London faded from my sight, their place was taken by a strange city of marvellous beauty and perfection. I saw stretching into illimitable distance a wide avenue of giant-figures of stone leading to a vast temple, of which every part had an astrological meaning. Formed like a circle, this temple appeared divided into twelve parts symbolising the Twelve Signs of the Zodiac and their influence on human life. In the middle of this majestic temple appeared a throne on which the Sun as the Giver of Life reigned in the form of a man-god. Rays of light charged with ions of magnetism radiated from this centre to each of the twelve signs and from them again flooded the Earth-Planet as it swept through each Sign in its annual pathway through the heavens. Stars sang to stars and suns to suns in one universal vibration of harmony.

Design, with threads of gold, linked planet to planet.

Purpose radiated from the Sun-God bearing Life and Death within its hands.

"How can Death be in the middle of Perfection?" I heard myself ask.

"Child of Man," the voice answered, "there can be no perfection without death. Death and Change are one—without change there would be stagnation. Creation and re-creation is the everlasting purpose of God."

The scene changed, the city became still more beautiful, the temple more magnificent. The wide space before the throne was filled with myriads of people, tall, straight, lordly, with the light of intelligence gleaming from their eyes, like gods or sons of gods they appeared.

I noticed that all were drawn by some mysterious magnetic force to the Sign of the Zodiac under which they were born; every man, every woman and every child was robed in the same colour as their Sign and on each forehead was their own distinctive jewel.

No brush could paint—no words describe—the splendour, the magnificence of such a scene. I felt I was called to witness the zenith of a people's grandeur and perfection.

"Child of Man," the voice spoke again. "Atlantis has reached its highest pinnacle, greater intelligence cannot be created, more knowledge cannot be attained. In this city there is neither disease nor crime. Men have become as gods, and being as gods, they bend their heads to Destiny."

In some mysterious way, two beings, a man and a woman, the most perfect of their kind, were drawn out of each of the twelve Zodiacal Signs. They appeared to receive some mission. They bowed their heads as they passed the Sun-God and as far as I could see, *they went from Atlantis to different portions of the earth.*

The Voice again spoke:

"Child of Man, thou seest before thee the Riddle of the Ages. Occult and astrological wisdom had taught these people the end of a period of civilisation was at hand, the end of twenty-five thousand years of progression, ascension and realisation. Through early centuries of strife, through wars, through myriads of religions they had come slowly upward to perfection—to fulfil their appointed span. As the butterfly lives but a day—the flower a week—man his three-score years and ten, and nations their centuries, civilisations must also pass away, and with the dawn of another 'precession' a new earth must also be born."

* * * *

The Sun-God had turned his face away, darkness rolled across the sky, wings of Death tinged with purple and gold loomed in blackening clouds and crashed in discord as they met.

The earth trembled and groaned—the City—a thing of beauty a moment before —now shivered like a human thing in agony.

The only light there was came from the temple where the souls of men and mortals bowed their heads in resignation—gods they had lived—*as gods they were prepared to die.*

From the North, oceans came thundering Southward. Icebergs met volcanoes in a clasp of death, Earth and Sea and Sky struggled for the mastery.

On the wings of Change, Death rode to triumph, and Atlantis the great, Atlantis the perfect, sank downwards to its doom.

* * * *

A shiver shot through my body—my spirit forced itself back. Instead of music a hideous discord had crashed through the room. The aerial was silent, the lights were out. I called to my friend—there was no answer—I groped my way to the organ—*the discord was explained*—exhausted with the long night's effort, he had fallen in a swoon across the keys.

FINIS